At Home Around the World

At Home Around the World

Elaine Townsend

Simona Gorton

CF4·K

10 9 8 7 6 5 4 3 2 1

Copyright © 2022 Simona Gorton
Paperback ISBN: 978-1-5271-0732-8
Ebook ISBN: 978-1-5271-0871-4

Published by Christian Focus Publications,
Geanies House, Fearn, Tain, Ross-shire,
IV20 1TW, Scotland, U.K.
www.christianfocus.com;
email: info@christianfocus.com

Cover design by Jeff Anderson
Cover illustration by Jeff Anderson
Printed and bound by Nørhaven, Denmark

Unless otherwise stated Scripture quotations are from The Holy Bible, English Standard Version, copyright © 2001 by Crossway Bibles, a publishing ministry of Good News Publishers. Used by permission. All rights reserved. ESV Text Edition: 2011.

Scripture quotations from the King James Version are marked with KJV.

Scripture quotations marked "TLB" or "The Living Bible" are taken from The Living Bible, Kenneth N. Taylor, Wheaton: Tyndale House, 1997, © 1971 by Tyndale House Publishers, Inc. Used by permission. All rights reserved.

All rights reserved. No part of this publication may be reproduced, stored in a retrieval system, or transmitted, in any form, by any means, electronic, mechanical, photocopying, recording or otherwise without the prior permission of the publisher or a licence permitting restricted copying. In the U.K. such licences are issued by the Copyright Licensing Agency, 4 Battlebridge Lane, London, SE1 2HX. www.cla.co.uk

Contents

Disaster! 7

Early Mischief 9

A Trip Around the World 21

A Shocking Realization 33

Miss Mielke 39

Budding Romance 49

The Crash 57

Lima and a Leper 67

Jungle Adventures 79

The Next Frontier 89

The Iron Curtain 95

Always Winter, Never Christmas 107

Arrested! 113

"Friendship" the Trailer 121

"Better Than We Dreamed" 133

Last Love 141

A New Mission 145

"Watch out, World!" 151

Unbeatable 161

Elaine Townsend Timeline 166

Thinking Further Topics 168

~ To my Whitney Elaine ~
May your heart be captured
with the same eternal Love
and may your light cause others to love
a beautiful Christ.

Disaster!

"Cameron, can you grab the sandwiches?"

Carrying a large basket and a small baby, Elaine walked toward the small plane as Cameron made one last trip across the dirt airstrip. At the plane, a group of around fifty people was gathered to see them off with prayers, songs, and hugs all round.

The year was 1947. Cameron and Elaine, along with six-month-old Grace, had been visiting "Jungle Camp" in southern Mexico to see how the new mission recruits were getting on. Jungle Camp was a three-month training for missionaries headed to remote areas. Here they would learn to create shelters out of branches and leaves without tools, ford rivers, hike primitive trails, treat snakebites, and survive with very little equipment of any kind.

Cameron and Elaine had stayed for three days, encouraging the young people, getting to know them and, of course, introducing everyone to baby Grace. Now it was time to return to Mexico City. The only plane available was a Piper Cruiser flown by a local commercial pilot. The seats had been removed for flying pigs to the city, earning it the appropriate nickname "pig plane."

Cameron climbed in first, then took the basket Elaine handed up with the baby, who was comfortably snuggled in among clean cloth diapers. Elaine stepped into the plane, but the door wouldn't close properly and she had barely fastened it shut before the plane was moving down the runway.

They both looked back through the windows, smiling and waving and straining for a last glimpse of their friends gathered behind them.

A few seconds later, Elaine turned to Cameron with a worried look. "Does something feel wrong to you?" Cameron looked down at the trees, noticing their odd angle.

They glanced forward at the pilot, who did not look as in control of his airplane as a pilot should be. Their hearts began to beat quickly, but there was no time to ask questions. The tail of the plane hit the tops of the jungle trees and dived, nose-first, into a ravine below. There was one moment of sheer terror as the ground raced toward the windows, then it was all over.

Early Mischief

Elaine was born in 1915 to a German printer named Herman and his wife, Lillie. Elaine's sister, Milly, was two years older, and their grandma, grandpa, aunt, and uncle also lived with them. Although the house was already full, Lillie kept an open house and visitors were frequent. Three big presses lived in the three car garage behind their home, and paper salesmen and customers were constantly coming and going. After supper, Lillie helped her husband run the hand-operated printing presses until around midnight. Together, they would print more than three million gospel tracts in their lifetime. However, customers didn't always pay on time and there were many mouths to feed.

Five days after her third birthday, World War II ended, but Elaine was busy with other problems. At two weeks old, she caught a cold, then stomach flu nine months later. She had sprained her wrist three times before she was three, then she caught another flu which affected her lungs, and scarlet fever which quarantined her for five weeks. Other episodes included a cracked elbow, measles, chickenpox twice, and falling down the stairs in her chair. Her father, a great lover of flowers, left a vase on her tray whenever she was sick—which apparently was often.

Herman had a wonderful sense of humor, and the older Elaine grew, the more it became apparent that she had inherited this trait. Five years after Elaine, Shirley was born, and Daniel arrived five years after her. Before Daniel was born, Elaine put a beach ball under her shirt and paraded around the neighborhood mimicking her mother and proudly telling everyone that she too was pregnant.

One day, when Elaine was in kindergarten, her mother heard a knock on the door. When she went to answer it, it was Elaine with her thirty-two classmates and two kindergarten teachers. "Mama!" Elaine exclaimed when a startled Lillie opened the door. "I brought everyone here to see our chicks!"

Another day Elaine pleaded with her father at the breakfast table, "May I run out and play!? I've finished all my chores!" Elaine's father looked out the window at the grey sky.

"Yes, you may play. But come in if it starts to rain. The hill gets slippery and you would probably fall. What would your mother say about a muddy dress!?" He winked at her and she darted off.

"And remember what I told you: only ride the tricycle on the sidewalk!"

A short while later, Lillie came running into the print shop— "Elaine has fallen! I think she might have broken her arm!"

Together they ran into the house where a chubby Elaine was cradling her arm and the rest of the family was gathered around. Elaine quickly looked up and, when she saw her father, said with a sheepish smile, "Don't spank me, dad, for I just broke my arm. I minded you—I did not go down the hill on the tricycle but went down in a wagon. And, if you do have to spank me for not minding you, please don't spank me on my arm."

* * *

The afternoon stretched along as humid Chicago heat blended with the colorful conversation carried on by the city. In one row house[1], Elaine lay on her stomach on the wood floor, kicking a door back and forth between her feet and reading a book. She guessed the end of the story, closed the book, and sat up.

Outside the screened doorway she could hear the metallic clatter and grate of her father's printing machine—a background noise never absent. Upstairs, footsteps meandered their way across the floor, and voices could be heard. In short, everyone was busy.

Elaine stood up and walked to the next room where Daniel and Shirley were playing. Or had been. Shirley now lay fast asleep on the floor, and Daniel hastened to present the appearance of tidying the room as he heard footsteps approaching, just in case they were his

---

1. A house which is attached to houses on either side.

mother's. At the sight of his sister, Daniel stopped and sat back on his heels.

"What are you up to?" she whispered, so as not to wake Shirley.

He shrugged.

Elaine sat down, picking up one of Shirley's books. She began to flip through it, then threw it down and crossed her arms, heaved a sigh, and turned on her back, staring at the ceiling. A second later she sat up. "Dan, how'd ya like to make some money?"

"You know the teacher says not to talk like that!" he retorted impudently.

She rolled her eyes and turned on her back again but kept watching him.

Curiosity won out, and Dan whispered back, "Fine."

Elaine had turned an idea over in her head for a long time (nearly an hour) and now seemed the perfect time.

She darted out the door, followed by her brother and a frustrated "What are you doing?"

At the front door she paused a second to listen and to think whether to take shoes. The sidewalk was hot. She grabbed her own shoes and hopped around while they took their time fitting on. Daniel did the same, and finally they both stumbled through the door together.

On the steps, she remembered something. "Stay here," she told Daniel. "And don't make one single noise."

Racing back up the steps, she listened an instant at the door, then slipped inside. When she reappeared, she handed a pewter cup to Dan and kept another for herself.

They raced down the street, and slowed to a stroll at the corner of the first intersection, a bit awed at being out on their own. A short while later, they reached a larger intersection and Elaine stopped. "Now," she explained to Dan, "try to look a bit sad. And hold out your cup."

Turning away from him, she faced the streams of people flowing all around them, and began to recite an inspirational poem:

> "I'm a poor little beggar girl
> My mother she is dead
> My father is a drunkard
> And won't give me no bread.
> I look out of the window
> To hear the organ play.
> God bless my dear mother,
> She gone far away.
> Ding-dong the castle bells ..."

Elaine slumped slowly down the light post behind her and turned a sly face to her companion, mostly to check his performance. He grinned back at her.

The next recitation of her poem met with a fresh audience since the crowds never slowed or stopped except to wait for a passing car. The coins began to pour into their cups. Things went along quite well, in fact, until a neighbor happened to spot the siblings and asked their mother, Lillie, if she knew where her children were.

At Home Around the World

* * *

When Elaine was seven, a terrible blow hit the Mielke family. Shirley squirmed on the doctor's table while receiving a diphtheria vaccine, causing the needle to hit her spine, and a crippling arthritis slowly made its way through her body over the coming years, incapacitating her by the end of her shortened life. While symptoms evolved, the first months were bewildering and all-consuming to Elaine's already overworked parents.

Still, that year Elaine, her mother, Milly, and Daniel were able to go on their annual church retreat at Moody's Cedar Lake Campgrounds. Elaine's father stayed home in muggy Chicago, working long hours and caring for Shirley, who screamed in terror at the thought of attempting the stairs to her bedroom. Herman wrote them letters while they were at camp—letters dreaming of a house in the country with a big yard, woods, and a creek where they could all play and not get run over by automobiles.

Four years later, Elaine was walking down the street and caught sight of an advertisement in the window of the bank her family used. It gave the offer of a special Christmas savings account, which Elaine decided would be a perfect way to save all her money for Christmas presents. So every Saturday from that day till Christmas, she marched over to the bank, a few blocks from her home, and made a deposit of twenty-five cents, which she had calculated would turn into thirteen whole dollars by December.

That next January, Elaine caught sight of another advertisement in the bank window. This time, in celebration of George Washington's birthday, the bank was holding a contest for the person who could make the most words out of the sixteen letters in his name. For the next two weeks, the Mielke family crowded around the dining room table on cold winter evenings with a pile of dictionaries, helping Elaine's list of words to grow. On February 22nd, Elaine proudly took her list of over 1,300 words to the bank and, unsurprisingly, she won. Her ten dollar prize was immediately deposited into her Christmas savings account.

But three years later, banks were not such a wonderful thing. A company had just paid Herman for a large job and he immediately took the $600 check to the bank. The next morning, the bank closed and all the Mielkes' money was lost. It was 1929: the beginning of the Great Depression.[2] Larger cities like Chicago took the hardest hits in this national crisis. Conveniences grew scarce, and the activities of life were reduced to necessity.

As the fall weather grew chilly, her mother called her into her room. "Elaine, we cannot afford to buy a new winter coat. You will have to wear this." And she pulled her grandpa's heavy military overcoat out of the closet.

"But mother!!" Elaine protested. "It's so ugly! All the girls at school will laugh at this. Milly got a new coat!"

---

2. The Great Depression was a worldwide economic collapse that lasted ten years and had far-reaching effects on the everyday lives of millions of people.

"Yes, but even hers is several sizes too big. Next year maybe we can get you a new one." Elaine was mortified.

It was around that time that Elaine spent an entire recess period trying on all the other girls' hats and got lice from one of them—she never knew which one. P.E. was her least favorite subject through high school, partly because she hated to change clothes and was built rather heavily. This battle with weight ran in the family and Elaine never outgrew the self-consciousness it brought.

The experience of these times formed habits that stayed with Elaine for the rest of her life. Her family might have been poor, but their faith was strong and she learned that happiness did not depend on having an abundance of money or clothes or food.

* * *

Lillie had always dreamed of teaching, but as that dream slowly faded due to tight finances, she passed on her natural talent to her daughters. She brought them along when she taught Sunday School at their church. Here, Elaine's lifelong affection for children and her passion for teaching began, as she watched her mother widen the eyes of a class in a circle on the floor to hear her retelling of God's tale.

One Sunday Lillie told a true story in Genesis of Satan tempting Adam and Eve. She explained, "God drove Adam and Eve out of the garden of Eden because of their disobedience. God gave them everything they needed to be happy, but they decided they knew better. That's when sin and hurt entered the world."

She turned to Elaine, "Could you hand out the pieces of paper?"

"Now children, draw a picture of God driving Adam and Eve out of Eden, then we'll come back together and look at your pictures."

A short while later, they gathered again and went around in a circle showing their pictures, but when it got to a little boy named David, everyone was a bit confused. On his paper there was a car with a man at the steering wheel and a man and woman in the back seat.

When Lillie asked him to explain his picture, he said confidently, "It's Jesus driving Adam and Eve out of the garden!"

* * *

From the time they were young, a sort of rivalry existed between Elaine and her sister, Milly. Milly learned most things naturally, while Elaine had to work harder for them. Still, it was Elaine who graduated from junior high at the head of her class. Elaine and her younger sister Shirley had a much warmer relationship.

After graduating from high school, Elaine decided to apply to Chicago Normal College, where Milly attended, to study teaching. Well-paying jobs were scarce during the Depression, but teachers were always in demand. However, Elaine "failed" the first entrance exam, because the head of the drama club was trying to get back at Milly for refusing to play the villain in a school play. Elaine only found out about this later.

Unable to attend college, the only job Elaine could find was at the Five and Ten dime shop a mile from home. Her earnings went to pay her family's mortgage payment. Without the technology available today, sales girls were a shop's most effective defense against theft. Elaine remembered pursuing at least one shoplifter on her three-inch heels, which were fashionable at the time.

When small boys were caught, the shop manager, Mr. Pence, dragged them downstairs where a large furnace was located. "Has no one ever told you that stealing is evil?", he would ask them, firmly holding them by their shirt collar. "I'll tell you, this is the last time you will ever think that grabbing yourself something for free from my shop is a good idea!"

He would then start up the furnace, which began to growl and bellow in a menacing way. "Now you have a choice," he would tell the frightened boy. "You have a choice between being thrown into this furnace or promising to go with Miss Mielke to Sunday School." They always chose Sunday School.

Two years later, Elaine retook the oral exam at Normal College and passed with flying colors—she had made the highest grade. For the next three years, Elaine rode the "L" (Chicago's elevated train) an hour and a half each way to attend classes at Normal College, where she eventually became president of the student council.

As a young adult, Elaine increasingly involved herself in the activities of Grace Evangelical Church.

In addition to playing the piano and teaching a Sunday School class, she helped with summer camps, midweek programs, Ladies' Aid meetings, church socials, and other events. She attended services every Sunday morning without fail, then returned at six in the evening for a young people's group and the evening service that followed. Eventually, she was elected president of Christian Endeavor and spoke at meetings. Along with a handful of girls she sang on a Christian radio station and performed at other churches.

She faithfully read through the Bible every year, and each summer at camp when an evangelist preached and invited people to come forward who wanted to believe in Christ, she was the first one up from her seat. In her heart she so desperately wanted to be sure that she was going to heaven, but she was never sure. She hoped that at the very least she could try to earn enough good points that God would let her in when she got there. It seemed logical enough. But she never felt satisfied, or even sure, that God loved her. No matter how hard she tried, she could never seem to do enough things right.

A Trip Around the World

When Elaine was twenty-one, the Chicago newspaper *Herald & Examiner*, ran an unusual contest to select the most devout Catholic[1], Jew[2], and Protestant[3] in the city. Thousands of churches and synagogues voted to select their candidate, then each would be interviewed at the Sherman Hotel downtown. Afterward, the top individual chosen in each of the three categories would win a trip around the world.

"Bye, everyone! Wish me luck!" Elaine hugged her father and waved to the rest of her family still clearing the dishes from dinner. She wrapped her coat around her and stepped out into a rainy, dismal Monday night. She and sixty-four other nervous young people made their way to the hotel—one of Chicago's historic landmark buildings—and were ushered into a room

---

1. Catholics believe the Pope and tradition are equal authorities alongside the Bible.
2. Jews do not believe Jesus is the Messiah and are still waiting for a Savior to rescue them.
3. Protestants believe that only by faith in Christ can we be saved from our sins.

At Home Around the World

with rows of chairs and a small room at one corner. She stared around her at the ornate wood paneling, floor-to-ceiling engravings, golden, luxuriant light reflecting off expensive chandeliers, and brilliantly colored carpet which seemed to extend for miles in every direction—every detail increased the surrealism of that moment.

A lady in a businesslike suit came out of the small room holding a clipboard: "Elaine Mielke!" she called. When Elaine came forward, she told her, "Your interview will be in this room and you will have fifteen minutes."

After her examination, Elaine sat for four hours, nervously waiting as contestant after contestant was ushered into the room where pastors and heads of theological seminaries questioned them and conferred among themselves. One young man behind her urged everyone to go home. "You all don't have a chance. They've practically chosen me already. I can feel it." But a pretty girl across the room in Salvation Army uniform caught Elaine's eye. Surely, she was the sort of person who would be chosen. Elaine looked down at her own dress and wished it was a few sizes smaller. All the same, Elaine considered, her record of service in the church was impressive.

At long last, the religious news editor for the newspaper emerged from the room with a piece of paper in his hand. Instead of immediately announcing the name of the winner, Dr. Anderson began describing the trip which the three winners would take (and unfortunately, he could describe everything in great detail). The group would sail from Montreal, Canada to the United Kingdom, then on to Northern Europe for the World Sunday School Convention in Oslo, Norway. After that, they would travel down through Europe to the Holy Land, and back again by sea to New York—a grand total of almost thirty cities, across fourteen countries, in seventy-eight days. The winner would journal regularly, take pictures (a novelty back then), and bring back news of their experience for all of Chicago.

When at long last he read the name of the Protestant winner, Elaine wondered if she had heard right. She sat for a long moment as the room erupted into applause. She got up from her seat in a daze and made her way up to the woman with the clipboard. "Is there a telephone here that I might use?"

After just two rings, Milly picked up the receiver.

"I won!" blurted Elaine, barely believing what she herself was saying.

After calling home, she stepped out into the street, eager to get back and tell her family and friends all about the evening. But she had forgotten about the rain, which had increased from a drizzle to a downpour while Elaine was in the hotel. She looked around for a paper which could serve as an umbrella and was about to pick up a *Chicago Daily*, then thought better of it and bought the day's issue of the *Herald & Examiner*.

At Home Around the World

A few days later, this same newspaper ran an article titled "Girl, 20, Wins Church Trip to Holy Land." It read, "At the end of the process, Miss Mielke's name was the first of a final group of five. Louise Jensen of the Salvation Army was second ..."

"Strangely enough," said Elaine years later, "they didn't pick up on the fact that I wasn't really a Christian."

And so it was that Kitty Levy, the daughter of a prominent rabbi in Chicago, Bud Jennings, who was studying for the priesthood, and Elaine Mielke, who confidently believed she was earning her way to heaven, began preparations for their almost three-month journey. Chicago would see the world through their eyes.

A Dean of Women at the Normal College lent Elaine $200[4] for clothing and she needed no further encouragement. The image of Elaine that appeared in the *Herald & Examiner*, ready to depart on the train for Montreal with Kitty, Bud, and Dr. Anderson was one of elegance and poise. "It took me about five years to pay her back, however," Elaine commented later.

* * *

The world of 1936 stood on the brink of epic changes and events. On a warm, bright day in June, Elaine, Kitty, Bud, Mr. Mee (one of the judges), and their chaperone, Dr. Anderson, sailed away from Canada on a vessel which would earn the title of "most bombed ship still afloat" after action in World War II.

---

4. Nearly $4,000 in today's currency.

Always at ease among people, Elaine threw herself into the social life aboard ship. She formed new acquaintances, danced, and enjoyed conversation with many sorts of people. One can only imagine the contrast she felt as she left her depression-era home to join pleasure seekers, students, businessmen, and people from many walks of life. During the trip she seemed to take on a new identity—one of fashion, importance, and the delights of the high life.

During their first night on land after eight days of sailing, Elaine woke to find two big green eyes staring her in the face. She screamed in terror and turned on the lights, waking Kitty, her roommate. The cat turned out to be harmless enough, but Elaine cried herself to sleep after it was all over. There were plenty more adventures ahead.

Elaine filled the pages of her diary with twelve-course dinners, eight-piece evening orchestras, the chores of packing, washing clothes, and comparing the size of silverware in each country. It became clear that she placed a great importance on fashion and looked down on those who were somewhat less refined. Dr. Anderson rarely acted the part of a chaperone, and on more than one occasion seemed to enjoy the nightlife a little too much himself. Elaine, Kitty, and Bud were left to go out as often as they chose, and Elaine, for one, did not complain. Luxury quickly became a welcome feature of life and they weren't shy to stay out on the town till all hours of the night.

At Home Around the World

In England they toured Westminster Abbey, made even more grand as it was in the middle of being prepared for the coronation of Albert George after the abdication of his brother, Edward VIII[5].

After arriving in Norway, they discovered that the Pension Atlas Hotel did not meet their approval. As they explored their room, Elaine glanced at Kitty. "This place sure is something! No running water or anything."

"So old fashioned!" Kitty exclaimed.

"The beds aren't bad, though. And look! Our bedroom is bigger than the hotel dining room."

The place didn't meet the standards of Dr. Anderson, however, and the next day the group relocated to the Grand Hotel—which lived up to its name. While in Norway, they were expected to attend the International Sunday School Convention, but Elaine used the free pass provided by the conference to ride the streetcar. Suddenly, Sunday began to seem like every other day to this girl. "I'd never missed a Sunday School or church," Elaine said later, "but now, all of a sudden, Sunday would come around and seem like any other day."

Just a border away from them was the Soviet Union. Elaine could never have imagined then, but the Soviet Union was a place which would become very familiar in years to come. They visited Berlin and the Garrison Church, where a new government had been inaugurated three years earlier by Adolf Hitler.

---

5. Edward VIII gave up the throne to marry his American girlfriend.

Eighteen days after they left Germany for Switzerland and the Middle East, Germany began one of her most magnificent acts of propaganda[6] to date: the 1936 Berlin Olympics. Hitler had designed the event to showcase the superiority of his "master race" and the entire city was cleared of anything offensive which would reveal to the rest of the world what his dark intentions truly were.

They stopped at Athens, Greece, then traveled through the Dardanelles and past Gallipoli[7] reaching Istanbul—the city of mosques, at sunset. Beirut was their next stop, then Syria, where they saw Damascus and the street called Straight where Paul the Apostle found the house of Ananias in the book of Acts. The next day they braved crowded streets and bazaars to visit Arabic shrines. Despite warnings about the current revolution, the group insisted on being taken to the area of Galilee. Elaine herself thought the dangers were probably imaginary.[8] They could not enter Capernaum, but they dipped their hands into the Jordan, and returned safely to Damascus.

Guided by a Syrian nobleman, they visited ruins which had been built by the Phoenicians in 1,000 B.C. then expanded into a series of temples by the Romans

---

6. Propaganda aims to influence people to believe something by discrediting the opposing viewpoint through a false or biased presentation of facts rather than through discussion.
7. Both of these places had become famous in WWI.
8. In April of that year riots and protests had broken out in Palestine between the Arabs and Jews. The threats were not imaginary.

during the Christian era. They returned to Jerusalem via Beirut and Haifa, but because of the unrest, their travel company refused to take them through Galilee and Samaria. Instead, they spent the night at the Stella Maria hospices, situated atop the Carmelite mountain range near the traditional site of Elijah's cave and operated by Carmelite monks. The hundred-mile journey along the Mediterranean coast disappointed no one.

From her window that evening, Elaine looked out over the bay of Acre—a place which had seen centuries of history all the way back to Roman times. Below her, the lights of Haifa shone like thousands of stars, and the light of the moon created an ethereal scene which was only intensified by the music of the crickets, the bells of the monastery, and the voices of the monks singing their vespers chants.

The next day, they prepared to visit the hills, valleys, and plains where Abraham, Moses, Solomon, David, and Jesus of Nazareth had walked.

The group took an armored train to Jerusalem next and visited the house of Caiaphas, the assumed site of the Last Supper, the Pool of Siloam, and Gethsemane on the Mount of Olives. However, they were prevented from visiting the Mount of Olives at moonlight since a curfew law allowed guards to shoot anyone who didn't respond to their call. After visiting the Dome of the Rock and Bethlehem, they took a train across the Gaza Desert, a ferry across the Suez Canal, and arrived in Cairo.

A sheikh named Mohammad accompanied them to the edge of the Sahara Desert the next morning, and they spent the day at the pyramids and Sphinx. On camelback, they arrived at the base of the Pyramid Chezrah, and Elaine recalled the words of Napoleon to his troops at this spot centuries earlier: "Gentlemen, at least forty centuries look down upon you."

The small party climbed the Great Pyramid of Giza, from which they looked 451 feet down to the sand, across the Sahara on one side and the green fields of the Nile on the other. They were told it took 100,000 slaves twenty years to complete the massive stone structure. From there, they visited the oldest Christian church of Cairo, built in the fifth century by Coptic Christians[9] over what they believed to be the house of the holy family during their flight from Bethlehem.

After Cairo and Alexandria, they sailed for Marseilles on the coast of France, then Rome, where they set out immediately for St. Peter's Basilica, the catacombs, the Coliseum, and the forum, then onto the Vatican library, and the Sistine Chapel. The merging of antiquity and modernity captivated them. But the highlight of their time—perhaps of the entire trip—came in the form of an audience with Pope Pious XI, arranged by a Cardinal in Chicago.

* * *

It was a tense group which assembled in the audience room and awaited the entrance of this man, the head

---

9. An ancient branch of Christianity dating back to the early Church.

of the Roman Catholic Church. The interview was intended to be private, but more than fifty people assembled with them in a line to be inspected by the guard. "All your heads must be covered, and if anyone has bare arms they must be wrapped in gauze!" A few moments later, footsteps were heard, then the sound of trumpets as heralds appeared in bright uniforms. When the Pope himself entered, everyone fell to their knees immediately—except Elaine. Bud, the Catholic, pulled at her skirt insistently. "Get down, Elaine! Get down or you will go to hell!"

Despite her lack of real faith, Elaine knew it wasn't right to bow before a man. During the entire experience, she felt a bit like Daniel standing boldly before the king of Babylon and refusing to bow down to his statue.

Some of Elaine's Catholic friends back in Chicago had given her rosaries for the Pope to bless however, so she stood dutifully in line. Each person approached, bowed slightly, and kissed his ring. Elaine's turn came and she put out her hand to shake his. He wasn't too happy, but he shook her hand. For the rest of her life Elaine would jokingly ask her friends, "Would you like to shake the hand that shook the Pope's?"

Paris was next, with all her brilliant sights, then the final part of thirty-eight days of sea travel, and New York. On her return to Chicago, Elaine visited dozens of churches, showing her black and white pictures and movies of her travels, which were quite a novelty.

Elaine Townsend

As she looked back on the trip, one experience in particular stood out in her memory—one she did not share with the churches she visited. While sailing across the Mediterranean, Mr. Mee came to join Elaine at the railing of the ship. They chatted for a few minutes, then he said, out of the blue, "You know Elaine, you really didn't win this trip. Do you remember that little Salvation Army girl?"

"Yes," she replied, startled. "I thought at the time that she would win."

"Well, she did. But we called her in after we had interviewed everybody and asked her if she would be willing to play cards and dance and leave her uniform at home. 'Oh no, I couldn't do that!' she replied. the *Herald & Examiner* wanted somebody who would be a good social mixer and we thought you would fit the bill."

"But you never asked me if I would do those things!"

"Oh, we knew you would—we could tell by looking at you."

Elaine turned away, crushed, and quickly found an way to excuse herself from the conversation. Apparently she seemed like the worldly type. She wanted to be liked, of course, but how could she get to heaven if she was known as a party girl?

The other girl on the trip, Kitty, had graduated at seventeen from the University of Chicago with a degree in anthropology before winning the trip around the world. A bright future shimmered out in front of her. While on the trip, however, she contracted a fatal illness and was dead a year later. Elaine felt a chill when she heard the news.

Another shock would soon strike deeper. The God of whom she knew so little, yet tried so hard to please, had set a course for her life more different than she could have ever dreamed.

A Shocking Realization

It was a quiet Sunday afternoon. After church, a few friends had come over for lunch. Now most of the family were reading while her mother prepared the Sunday School lesson for the next week and Milly popped corn.

Lillie looked up. "Elaine, would you be able to pick up Shirley from her Bible Study this evening? It's pouring outside and I don't want Shirley walking home in this weather."

"Sure!" Elaine responded and went back to her book. A little while later she put on her coat and stepped out into the drizzly evening.

While Elaine was in Europe, her brother Daniel had begun attending the North Side Gospel Center, and although the family had faithfully attended church for years, he felt convicted under Lance Latham's preaching like never before. Shirley, too, would later point to this church as the means of her conversion, and together they became involved in this community of believers. The church had once been a bowling alley only two blocks from their home, but Shirley was not sure on her feet, especially with the gusty rain blowing that evening. "Church in a bowling alley?" Elaine had thought when she first heard about it.

A few minutes went by, then a few more. Still, Shirley didn't appear. At last a pretty girl came out, wearing a beautiful gray squirrel coat. "She does know how to dress!" Elaine thought to herself. "This place must not be too shabby after all." She decided to go inside and see for herself.

Inside was a crowd of young people with lively music playing. A few came up and greeted Elaine. It felt different than her own church with its established cliques. People stayed after the study to talk and she noticed that they treated the crippled Shirley with friendliness and ease. Elaine gladly accepted an invitation to a hayride and harvest party, then a Tuesday night Bible class.

That Tuesday, she walked in and saw two groups of girls gathered around ping pong tables and some boys in another room. The girls looked up and smiled. What Elaine didn't know was that Daniel and Shirley had asked their groups to pray for their sister's salvation—her, the "best Protestant" in all Chicago.

Virginia Latham, the pastor's wife, was teaching from Leviticus. When Elaine appeared, Virginia immediately began thinking about how she could present the gospel through the text. She had been told that Elaine was a very sophisticated girl, but she also knew that the answer to her needs was the same as any other person, so she silently prayed, trusting Elaine to the power of the Word itself.

They read about the Day of Atonement and began to discuss the text. "You see," said Virginia, "the blood of Christ is our only way to heaven. Girls," she said, leaning forward, "do you realize what this means? Baptism has nothing to do with your salvation. Nor does confirmation."

Elaine's mind began to race.

"Nor does giving your tithe or church membership," Virginia continued. "None of these things will get you to heaven."

A pause. Finally, Elaine spoke up: "Mrs. Latham, I can't prove to you where you're wrong, but if you will come and talk to my pastor he can show you where it says you have to have these things to get to heaven."

Virginia—"Teach" as she was affectionately dubbed by the girls—held up her well-worn Bible and said, "Elaine, if I can prove to you that what I have been telling you is God's plan for salvation, would you believe it?"

"Go ahead and try—show me one verse in the Bible that proves it," Elaine challenged.

"Girls, open up to John 1:12-13."

"'But to all who did receive him, who believed in his name, he gave the right to become children of God, who were born, not of blood nor of the will of the flesh nor of the will of man, but of God.'"

Virginia turned to Elaine, "Where does it say that infant baptism, giving your tithe, perfect church attendance, and all the rest of your good works will save you?"

Elaine read the verse over silently: "... as many as receive him ..."

"Well, I don't see it here, but give me another verse."

Teach didn't miss a beat: "Turn to John 5:24."

"'Truly, truly, I say to you, whoever hears my word and believes him who sent me has eternal life. He does not come into judgment but has passed from death to life.'"

"What tense is that verb?"

"It sounds like something that is true right now."

"That's right. What do you think that means?" A moment of silence followed. All the girls buried their faces in their Bibles, waiting to hear what Elaine would say.

But it was Teach who eventually answered her own question: "The crazy thing is, that means you can know here, right now, whether you are saved. If you believe that Jesus' work on the cross covered your sins, you can know you are going to heaven with Him."

Elaine still wasn't satisfied. "So works don't count for anything to get us to heaven?" It was beginning to seem that in all her years of faithfulness she had missed the key on which all the gospel turned. Was it possible? Elaine had come to the Bible study that evening on a whim, but now she found herself wishing she hadn't. This was all very uncomfortable, and she felt with consternation as though the street on which she lived their entire life had vanished. Something odd was building inside her. A sinking feeling, yet it was strangely like hope.

"Turn to Romans 4:4-5 next," Virginia continued.

"'Now to the one who works, his wages are not counted as a gift but as his due. And to the one who does not work but believes in him who justifies the ungodly, his faith is counted as righteousness.'"

Virginia spent the rest of the evening bringing Elaine through the Scriptures and proving to her that nothing she did could earn her salvation; instead, it was completely free. Free to be grasped by faith alone.

When Virginia asked her to read Ephesians 2:8-9, Elaine could hardly believe her eyes.

"'For by grace you have been saved through faith. And this is not your own doing; it is the gift of God, not a result of works, so that no one may boast.'"

"Am I reading it right?" she wondered. The road by which she thought she could get to heaven turned out not to lead there after all. There was a struggle in her soul. She reached breaking point: she was not good, and she could not satisfy a holy God.

"Not a result of works …" That's exactly what I'm doing, trying to earn heaven by my own goodness.

"… the gift of God …"

"It was like turning on a light," she said later.

Her eyes lit up and joy illuminated her face. "I see it now!" she murmured, quietly. "It's so clear, so wonderful—it's too good to be true! There's certain hope for me in heaven if I trust in Christ."

At the point of desperation, in the realization of sin and justice, the Spirit broke through. "It was the Word that got me," she said later. And indeed, it could have been nothing less. The verses she read that day were indelibly pressed upon her mind and from then on she was captive. God had won out at last over all her worried, guilt-driven efforts.

Not even waiting to pray with the group, Elaine ran home to the shop behind her home where her father was hard at work printing gospel tracts. "Dad, stop the press!" she exclaimed. "Did you know you can be sure of your salvation while you're still here on this earth?"

"Sure I knew that." he replied. "Didn't you?"

"But Dad, you never told me that!'

"Well, aren't you listening to the messages? I see you go to church all the time—don't you listen? Aren't you hearing? Aren't you writing notes? I've seen you writing notes about the sermon, so I thought you knew the Lord."

"I'm writing notes," Elaine replied, "but I've never understood before. I've always wanted to know whether I was saved for certain, but no one ever told me that it was all the Lord's work."

Miss Mielke

Elaine graduated from Teachers' College at the top of her class, earning the privilege of being the first to choose the school where she would teach. Much to her classmates' shock, she chose one in a rough Chicago neighborhood, and walked in the first day to discover that many of the students who were older hadn't been moved to the next class and were completely out of hand. They spent the day swinging from the pipes along the ceiling of the classroom and Elaine spent the day pulling them down, only to return home demoralized and exhausted each night. Finally, the older students were moved to another class and things calmed down a little.

Each day at lunch, Elaine read her Bible, and one day a student approached her. "Are you ever going to finish that book?"

"Alex, I'm never going to finish this book."

"But why do you like it so much?"

"Listen," Elaine told him, "you go around and if all the boys and girls want to know why I like it so much, I'll tell you."

At Home Around the World

From that moment, he became her press agent: "You guys want to know what she's reading, don't ya?'"

Every afternoon from then on, a group of children—many of them abused or disabled—gathered for Elaine to tell them stories which brought alive a loving God so few of them knew.

Around that time, Elaine also started a mission for the local Mexican children, scrubbing out a filthy shopfront building from top to bottom and holding after-school gatherings. She even began to learn Spanish so she could give Bible lessons.

One day, the woman who taught Elaine Spanish told her about a speaker she had heard the evening before—Cameron Townsend. His new organization, Wycliffe Bible Translators, ran a program called the Summer Institute of Linguistics (SIL) in Norman, Oklahoma, which taught the skill of reducing oral languages[1] to writing.

Elaine hadn't even heard of Wycliffe before and had very little idea of how challenging linguistics work was, but Ann's excitement was contagious: "I'm going this summer! Why don't you come with me?" Elaine jumped at the chance, and soon they were off to spend school break attending SIL linguistics camp.

It was a wonderful summer.

Little did she know that the next year the course would be shut to any not considering full time mission work—which she certainly was not!

---

1. Languages which are only spoken and have no written form.

While Elaine was at SIL camp, the staff were praying for someone to teach missionary children so the wives could help their husbands with the work of translation. Elaine began to realize how much this could speed up the work of Bible translation, so at one point she leaned over to a classmate, "Esther! I think you should go!"

"Don't pray for me, Elaine! I hate teaching school."

From that time on, Elaine heard the question in her mind: What about me?

And so the battle began.

When she returned to Chicago at the end of the summer, her talent for teaching had been recognized and she was made the supervisor over the special-needs programs in 300 schools. At twenty-six, she was the youngest supervisor and the first woman ever appointed to this position by the Chicago school district. The salary wasn't bad either.

She told the Lord it would be impossible for her to go to the mission field to teach children. She was happy to give her money, but it would be ridiculous to waste a good opportunity. "You don't want me," she told Him.

For a year, she struggled with a nagging sense that God was calling her to go to the field. She feared that if she did, three things would happen: she would have no friends, she would always be single, and she would probably become terribly ugly.

One night, she could stand the burden no longer. She shut herself in the bathroom (the only room in the house with a lock) and determined not to come out until she had made a decision. She wrestled with the Lord and against His call on her life. She had something very different in mind and could not envision what His plan would look like.

When she emerged in the early hours of the morning, a new resolve for obedience had taken hold of her. She had let go of her own desire for recognition and comfort. If the Lord had called her, she must go. Her Jesus was worth far more than all her dreams.

As her friends and co-workers expressed surprise at this decision, appearing so sudden, Elaine told them that the Lord had called her to serve Him in Mexico. Still, she felt sure that her three fears would come true.

At the train station, around fifty of her Mexican friends and all her family came to see her off. They cried and sang hymns together and soon, the train began to move, going south toward the border and Mexico.

* * *

In June of 1943, with her homeland in the middle of World War II, Elaine entered Mexico. The plan was for her to teach missionary children for six months, then work with the indigenous[2] people for six months to develop new visual education techniques.

She and another SIL recruit, Ethel, arrived in Mexico City eager to begin work. SIL owned a modest group house, but the girls considered even that too luxurious, so they rented a small bedroom on the first floor of a cheap hotel. The next morning, they woke

---

2. Local Indian tribes living in the region.

up at noon to discover they had been drugged to sleep and all their possessions stolen.

Suddenly deciding the cost was affordable, the two girls moved into the SIL group home shortly afterward, and it became a place of rich fellowship, good conversation, and much laughter. Not surprisingly, Elaine was soon popular among the group.

After a few months of intensive language study, Elaine moved to the Aztec village of Tetelcingo, about sixty miles south of Mexico City. Here, Cameron and his wife, Elvira, also lived, working with the indigenous people on practical projects like bringing water into the village, teaching the women to sew, and starting vegetable gardens in the town square. Cameron also created an alphabet and developed reading material for the local language. President Cárdenas of Mexico had a great respect for their work and he and Cameron were good friends.

In Tetelcingo, Elaine found a grand total of three children ready to be her pupils, and no schoolroom. In these first months, she sometimes struggled with discouragement, but she tried to throw herself into the work and the children who needed her. Those pupils would remember her adventurous field trips years later.

Elaine's trip around the world had given her a keen interest in other people and cultures. From Mexico she wrote many letters home to her family, painting for them a lively picture of colorful surroundings. The streets were narrow and the sidewalks crowded. People along the street held up puppies, colorful fabrics, and

At Home Around the World

many other wares for purchase. On Flag Day, Elaine joined in the celebrations, which included six bands which sounded to her as if they were all trying to play a different tune at the same time.

In addition to teaching, Elaine helped Elvira with office work and cultivated relationships with other missionaries. She saw a need for a Sunday School, so she and one of the local boys went from hut to hut inviting people. These gatherings were well attended by around fifty people—women, children, and some intrigued men.

Her home in Tetelcingo was a little clay adobe[3] house which she soon made into a welcoming place. She loved to have company, and quickly began to show her care and love for others by taking everyday opportunities to encourage others around her table.

Elaine had thought that being a missionary only involved loneliness and sacrifice, so she brought many books to fill the long hours. She was quickly proved wrong. Life became fascinating and there was much to fill her days. To her great surprise, she found that even in this strange country so far from home, with its disappointments and setbacks, her heart was satisfied and joyful.

* * *

As she neared the adobe hut of Doña Juana, Elaine could hear the pleasant pat, pat, pat of her hands

---

3. Adobe is a red clay which dries hard like bricks and is commonly used to build houses in South America.

shaping tortillas, mingled with the sound of a baby crying. There was no doorbell, so she called "Buenos días, Doña Juana!" and was invited in. After offering her a little piece of wood on which to sit, Doña Juana hurried back to her work.

Elaine played with the baby and tried her hand at helping to grind corn, then explained that she had come to teach Doña Juana some games. The cards were brightly colored and immediately attracted her interest. This was likely the first time that Doña Juana had been asked to play a game since she was married at the age of twelve. Slowly, she began to recognize letters and sound them out. Elaine worked with her for a little while, then moved on to the next hut to teach another friend and pupil.

For some time, Cameron had been working to develop teaching techniques to help indigenous people from remote tribes learn to read. When missionary translators entered a tribe, their first goal (after creating a written language if it was oral), was to teach the village to read. This could be incredibly challenging and would usually take years. Elaine was gifted with a particular spark and energy which engaged her listeners for hours. This proved invaluable in Wycliffe's work to bring literacy to isolated tribes and, ultimately, give them the Word of God in their own heart language.[4]

---

4. A person's heart language is the language they first learn as a child. To translate the Bible, missionaries often have to create a written alphabet for a particular tribe and teach them to read before they can even begin the work of Bible translation. The entire process can often take up to thirty years.

At Home Around the World

After her first year of teaching missionary children, Elaine launched a year-long reading campaign for the Aztecs in Tetelcingo and traveled by train, bus, and mule to remote villages across Mexico. She worked closely with the local translators, teaching them to teach as she held classes for the local men, women and children using simple words and conversational phrases like: How are you? What's your name? Do you have any children?

First, though, she needed a place to teach. She soon learned that if she started with the children or the women, the men would think the classes were silly. So she marched right into the town tavern and began classes for the men, who immediately liked the pretty, smart woman who came to teach them.

However, the women had often been told how stupid they were and Elaine had to work at developing relationships and encouraging their confidence. Once sufficient trust had been earned, Elaine could organize classrooms where rowdy children shouted answers and chickens and lizards made themselves at home. The indigenous people loved to sing, so Elaine started teaching them how to read and sing hymns, rich with gospel truth, and they became eager for the Word. The Spirit worked and some reading pupils became believers in the true and living God.

In one remote village, a cyclone destroyed all bridges and Elaine and her traveling companion were cut off from communication with the outside world.

Rumors spread that the indigenous peoples' gods had sent the storm to punish them for letting the "white witches" live among them. Elaine and the other missionaries spent a few tense weeks hearing reports of killing and looting in neighboring villages, but they remained unharmed.

Throughout her travels, Elaine observed the joyful spirit of the missionaries she met and worked alongside. Despite much hardship, they saw it as a privilege to work in God's service and carry the good news to the people among whom they lived. Elaine was deeply impacted by these men and women.

Budding Romance

The year after Elaine arrived in Mexico, Cameron's wife, Elvira, passed away. Like her husband, she had been passionate to see the gospel's growth among the tribes of Mexico, but she was plagued by heart and mental illnesses for which there was little help at the time. During Cameron's frequent trips, she and Elaine had developed a close friendship and Elaine learned much from this more experienced missionary.

After Elvira's death, many of the team speculated about whether Cameron would remarry and, without her knowing, Elaine was secretly elected as the most likely candidate by five separate groups. Unfortunately, she had decided a long time ago that she would not marry someone much older than herself, and Cameron was nineteen years older. She was unprepared for God's sense of humor.

Cameron was known as "Uncle Cam" to all the missionaries. One day in conversation, he asked if Elaine would leave off the "Uncle" part. Then he turned down an invitation to an evening of chess with a friend to help Elaine make curtains for her bathroom. He began to take the opportunities provided by so many people trying to put them together and didn't seem to mind.

As love began to spark and their travels kept them frequently apart from one another, they wrote letters back and forth. "Only twenty-nine hours have elapsed since you left us," Cameron wrote, "but I find myself longing to be near you again. Your presence, however, has seemed to be hovering around. Everyone here has mentioned how they enjoyed you—how lovely you are."

Despite a growing relationship, Cameron struggled to discern whether marriage was indeed God's will for their lives. He was deeply aware of the difference in their ages and wondered if it was inconsiderate to pursue Elaine. Elaine herself had much to consider. Cameron and Elvira had been unable to have children, so if she and Cameron married it was a possibility that they would not be able to have a family. Cameron's frequent travels and extensive responsibilities would make home life difficult, and it was likely that she would be caring for him as he aged. Yet they were both fully committed to the mission of reaching unreached tribes[1] with the Word of God and knew that this would be the guiding passion of any life together.

---

1. Unreached people groups "lack enough followers of Christ and resources to evangelize their own people" and often do not have God's Word in their own language. (www.joshuaproject.net, accessed on 3/21/21)

Elaine Townsend

While Elaine was in Chicago visiting family, she received a telephone call.

"Temitztlasohtla meac," she heard on the other end of the line.

"Pardón?" Elaine replied in Spanish.

"Temitztlasohtla meac," Cameron repeated.

She wasn't exactly sure what he had said, so she thanked him and hung up. Later, she realized it was Cameron telling her he loved her in Aztec.

Their letters proved that even missionary romance, submitted to God above all, was anything but boring. "I'm hopelessly in love," wrote Cameron. "There's no doubt about that. By the grace of God, however, that love is going to remain sanctified to Him, though I can see that I'm going to need your constant help in this regard. He must always come first, even in this."

Gradually, after months of wrestling, they both came to believe that they could honor God through marriage better than they could if they remained single. Once engaged, they were the news of the base, with many of the missionaries believing they were the ones responsible for such a good match!

In an attempt to be prudent, Cameron decided they should wait two years before marrying, but a close friend laughed off the idea. "Don't be silly, Townsend! A wonderful girl like that? She would make a tremendous difference at the mission base you're working to get started in Peru. It just doesn't make sense. It seems to me that anyone marrying a tremendous woman like

Elaine would want to spend as many years of his life with her as he could! Who would want to wait?"

The date was set for March of 1946. Japan surrendered to the allies in September and the whole world, it seemed, breathed a sigh of deep relief. The coming months would be fruitful ones for the work of Wycliffe and SIL. Elaine continued her reading campaigns across Mexico while Cameron led training at Jungle Camp and planned the wedding himself—with only one significant mistake.

President Cárdenas of Mexico and his wife invited Cameron and Elaine to hold the ceremony at their country estate, and many prominent officials were invited as well. The Cárdenas family spared no expense: a full orchestra played the dinner music, hundreds of flowers decorated the walls, and the cake was over three feet high—so tall they had to take out one of the windows to bring it into the room.

Elaine's sister, Shirley, had worked hard to learn Spanish so she could communicate with everyone she would meet at the wedding. Throughout Elaine's time on the mission field, Shirley would be one of her closest friends and confidants, praying faithfully and writing every Sunday. Despite her ongoing battle with arthritis, she was a beautiful woman with brown, sparkling eyes who engaged people in lively conversation everywhere she went.

The night before the wedding, Cameron spent hours talking and sharing the gospel with President

Cárdenas, his close friend of many years. The big day went off without a hitch until the wedding was over and Cameron suddenly turned to Elaine. "I just realized what I forgot!"

"It couldn't be too terrible! Everything has been lovely," she replied, squeezing his arm and giving him a kiss.

"No, I forgot to reserve a room for our first night together."

In the end, a friend gave up his hotel room so Cameron and Elaine had a place to sleep.

* * *

The love that was inaugurated that day would last their lifetime—through highs and lows, many countries, and much gospel service. Elaine became Cameron's great encourager. "When Elaine came," said one friend, "it was like the reinforcement of the troops." Their letters were playful and full of affection and flirtation. "Hi Dill Pickles!" Cameron began one letter, then added "that doesn't sound as complimentary as I want it to but I am sure that you understand, knowing how much I love dill pickles."

Life together started off at full speed. In Mexico City, the missionaries at the group house had filled their room with prank "decorations" to welcome them back. This place possessed all the beauty and hilarity of a vibrant community. An old mansion-style hotel had been divided into living spaces for a number of families, and affectionately dubbed "The Kettle." Many used this house as a stopping-off point before entering their jungle outpost, or as a station for refreshment after a long period in the bush. It became so packed that single men slept on mattresses in the storage room. Children ran in and out between the curtained rooms playing hide and seek, and groups of men and women spent hours in conversation, reading, and prayer together. On Sunday nights, everyone came together to share reports from the village where they were stationed—that was the part everyone looked forward to the most.

It was into this flurry of life that the newly-married Townsends arrived. Two women, Gloria and Ellen, performed a skit mimicking the two of them with affectionate good humor. Gloria dressed up as Elaine, dressed up nice with earrings, a brooch, a skirt, and of course, heels, telling everyone proudly, "Look girls! I've lost ten pounds!" Ellen was Uncle Cam, and the two of them pretended to be in love like Cameron and Elaine.

From Mexico City, the Townsends left for Peru. In Lima, they used their wedding money to rent a ten-bedroom house for a group of new recruits who would be arriving soon. The accommodations were makeshift once the house was full, with not enough furniture to go around, and a bout of food poisoning made things even more interesting. Elaine was kept rather busy caring for everyone as one of the few who escaped it.

Shortly after moving to Peru, Elaine was asked by the Peruvian government to develop reading materials and to lead reading campaigns for several remote tribes.

She began packing for the trip as fifty thousand copies of a primer she had written were printed. Of course, the General of the Peruvian Military Academy who was curious about their work in the city decided now would be a perfect time to come visit. Just hours before she left, the ambassador and his mother also showed up at the door. Elaine dropped everything and showed them around, explaining the teaching material she used and giving them one of her primers. On leaving, the ambassador promised to help get copyrights for her work.

Her travels would take her to the border of Bolivia, which was at a very high altitude and quite cold. This made breathing and sleeping difficult, yet Elaine thrived, and her classes with fifty-six native supervising teachers went well. They were so eager to learn that they hardly stopped for meals and would stay up at night studying what Elaine had taught them, so they could return to their cities and share the material with other groups of teachers. International education experts would declare Elaine's literacy materials some of the finest they had seen in the country.

"How I praise the Lord for this wonderful opportunity to help them!" she wrote to Cameron, "as it means that thousands of children and adults will be learning to read in Quechua and Aymara, and will be prepared to read the Bible just as soon as [the translations] come off the press."

At Home Around the World

But other things were happening as well—Elaine was pregnant with their first child! In the months before the birth, Cameron was scouting remote areas of Peru for a suitable place to establish a mission base. On December 27th, four days before President Truman of the United States officially declared the end of World War II and while Cameron was traipsing around the jungle, Grace Lillie Townsend made her appearance—two weeks early.

Upon his return to Lima, Cameron arranged a dedication ceremony for Grace at the Mexican Embassy, inviting around fifty friends. He and others prayed for this little girl, that she would grow in her love for the Lord and in her knowledge of His Word.

A few days later, the entire family departed for Mexico and Jungle Training Camp.

The Crash

Jungle Training Camp was a three-month exercise in survival. Many of the Wycliffe recruits were headed for remote areas where there was little or no connection to the outside world, and the nearest town with medical care could be days' or weeks' travel away. During this Camp, they went on long hikes, learned how to start fires, hunt for food, build shelters without tools in the wilderness, treat life-threatening illnesses, navigate whitewater rapids with a loaded canoe, learn to speak and write difficult languages, and many other skills they would need. Cameron had initially organized the training, but now it was led by other experienced missionaries, doctors, and linguists.

It was as the plane took off on the return trip that things went terribly wrong.

The frightened group who had just a few moments before waved them off with smiles raced to the scene of the crash. But someone was there before them. Baby Grace had been taken from the plane by an unknown Indian man and placed in safety. He was never seen afterward.

It was a miracle that everyone in the plane escaped with their lives. The pilot (a commercial hire) had been out in a bar drinking the night before and boasted to his companions that he would be the next of seven crashes in the valley that month. He also failed to turn off the gas switch when they started going down, so the plane should have gone up in flames—but it didn't.

When he recovered consciousness, Cameron asked about his wife and daughter, then said urgently to the nearest person, "You! Grab a camera! Take a few pictures of the plane. And of us."

For years he had been trying to persuade the Wycliffe board that missionaries needed their own pilots and airplanes, but at the time, these were luxuries, and missionaries didn't need luxuries, as he was repeatedly told.

It was the pictures from that crash which finally convinced the board and brought donors to help fund the beginning of Jungle Aviation And Radio Service (JAARS) which continues today to provide transport, communication, and other logistical services for missionaries around the world.

When Dr. Culley left Wheaton to direct Jungle Camp that year, he had no idea the drugs and medicine he packed in his bags would be likely saving the lives of Cameron, Elaine and the pilot of that unfortunate flight. For ten days he cared for them until he declared them ready to be transported out of the village.

Back in Mexico City, Cameron and Elaine lay on their backs in recovery for six months. Grace rotated between different families and was brought to visit once a day. When a young boy was tasked with cleaning their room, Cameron persuaded him to read the Bible aloud to them. The Spirit worked and through reading the Word every morning he came to call on Christ as his Savior.

God brought good fruit from this disaster, but the cost was high. Elaine wondered to herself whether this was the end of their ministry work. The front seat of the plane had collapsed on her feet, crushing them completely.

As in the first months at Tetelcingo, Elaine suffered from deep discouragement. She began to doubt if God's plan in this was truly best for her, for Cameron, for the work of Wycliffe. As the Bible was read to her one morning, a particular verse stood out: "It is good for me that I was afflicted, that I might learn your statutes" (Psalm 119:71).

She thought, could it really be good for me to go through all this agony?

Finally, after days of prayer and wrestling she said to the Lord, "Alright, if you think it's good for me, I'll believe it"—and that changed everything.

Many doctors said she would never walk again, and though she did, she would suffer significant pain for the rest of her life and require special shoes. Cameron's leg had undergone severe cuts and a permanent metal

At Home Around the World

plate had to be inserted. They would carry the scars of this experience with them for the rest of their lives, but the lesson of surrender Elaine had learned during those endless days would be a sweet fruit of grace, which would hold true through many hard experiences ahead.

* * *

Back on their feet, the Townsends visited family, friends, and ministry partners in the States, as well as missionaries and colleagues in Mexico, and began to set up their home in the jungles of Peru. Joy Amalia joined the family on Cinco de Mayo (the biggest Mexican holiday), while they were in Mexico and all the doctors were out celebrating. Cameron had to go search the streets for someone to help his wife deliver their second daughter.

The place Cameron had found for their house was a remote outpost on the shores of Lake Yarinacocha. It was a spot of thick jungle at the end of a six-mile-long, red clay road. The nearest town was very small and their neighbors were the Shipibo tribal people. Back in Lima, Cameron and Elaine had ripped apart surplus army tents from the war, then sewed them, along with generous amounts of mosquito netting, into one giant tent for their home. The shape of the tent was an "L," divided into three "rooms" and a tree in the middle where Grace and Joy slept on a platform. "We have much to do yet in getting settled," Elaine wrote home to her family in Chicago, "but it is lots of fun and much more comfortable than I had supposed it could be. As I write this I am looking out over a beautiful, quiet lake and a gorgeous sunrise."

Life in the jungle was a constant adventure—sometimes too much of one! While changing a diaper one day, Elaine found a scorpion hidden in its folds—baby Joy certainly would have died if she had been bitten. They once had an infestation of frogs for two months and Joy toddled around throwing them out of the house. She wouldn't touch the dried-up dead ones, however.

A businessman in the States saw a picture of Elaine and the girls dressed up in their best, smiling in front of their tent home. He immediately sent a $2,500 check for a "proper home." Elaine had the gift of making any place feel welcoming. In their new home, she set up metal travel trunks with a slanted board for the backrest and a crocheted blanket over the top for their living room couch. Two weeks after moving into their new jungle home, Elaine hosted sixty missionaries before they returned to their tribes across Peru.

Slowly, other men and women, pilots, mechanics, teachers, grocers, and others began moving to the base, building their homes, and establishing a flourishing community. Everyone was there for a common purpose: the goal of bringing God's Word to every tribe and language and people, no matter how rich or poor. To do this, they all made tremendous sacrifices. They were from diverse places and backgrounds, yet they came together here in this outpost along with their children—all adjusting to a new language and culture.

The base at Yarina had more conveniences than the smaller outposts deeper into the jungle where a couple, family, or two singles worked to make alphabets for oral languages, taught the indigenous people to read, then began the painstaking process of translating the Bible. A process that took three decades or more. Yarina was a place they could all come for refreshment and encouragement, as well as supplies, medical care, and communication with the outside world.

The atmosphere at Yarinacocha was one of celebration amid much hard work. People found every excuse for getting together or throwing a party. Every Friday night, families on the base gathered for games, skits, talent shows, recitals, and singing. One Sunday morning, Cameron played "Do the Bunny Hop" over the loudspeaker to alert the base that it was almost time for church.

Soon there was a shop, a school, a post office, and even a landing strip built onto the lake. The limitations of travel and stretched funds meant that families deep in the jungles often didn't know when they would see their relatives in the States again. Many who married on the base weren't able to have family come to their weddings.

Living conditions at Yarina were primitive. Appointments to use the base's radio service had to be made two weeks in advance. When the Townsends' home finally got water, it was pumped up from the lake, complete with tadpoles. Many outposts in the Peruvian jungle remained isolated, including military camps and Catholic missions. Elaine frequently sent packages of homemade bread, cookies, pickles, and produce with the pilots who stopped off at these settlements along their routes.

To increase people's understanding of Bible translation and the work of SIL and Wycliffe, Cameron designed visiting weeks for Ambassadors and Ministers of State, as well as other officials, educators, and news teams to experience life on the base. They had lunch with teachers on the base, took boat rides on the lake, visited an Indian village, gained firsthand experience of the SIL linguistics program, and shot at balloons with blowgun darts. They stayed, of course, in the Townsends' and others' homes on the base.

As it grew, Elaine quickly became the mother of the base, inviting new missionaries over for tea, hosting Sunday dinners, organizing a ladies' exercise time, and "lending" her attic to someone who needed a quiet place to write—then later to someone who needed to build a boat! She helped newcomers feel welcomed, included, and became known as a "gracious pioneer" as one person called her.

One year, nine hundred guests came through their doors for dinner, and four hundred and fifty of those spent the night. Elaine always loved to keep track of the numbers. Friends were always welcomed as family, and strangers soon became friends. They didn't have much to offer, but they didn't let that keep them from welcoming whoever came by. When a guest from the Ministry of Education accidentally cracked his fork trying to cut a cheap, tough cut of meat, everyone burst out laughing and Cameron commented to Elaine afterward, "Well at least they know we're not a lot of rich Americans coming to earn money!"

The Townsend home at Yarinacocha acted as a representation of the larger work of Wycliffe in many countries, and countless people caught a vision for the noble and massive undertaking of linguistics and translation through observing the gospel's power to forge a vibrant community even in the middle of the jungle. The homes of the base became its heartbeat as warm fellowship broke down walls of culture and adorned the gospel in a way unique to each home.

On one occasion, three men from an oil camp nearby came to visit the base. They remarked on the joy of the people at Yarina, even though it lacked the modern conveniences of their own camp. Both groups consisted of Americans living in a foreign country with more or less the same educational background. Yet one was discontent and grasping, the other joyful and spirited. One group saw money as their goal, the other sacrificed money and self to help others, "and it was the Word of God that made the difference," Elaine said.

Once when they were expecting three ambassadors and some officials from the Ministry of Education, a friend came to help with dinner preparations. "Would you get my china out and just put it on the table?" Elaine asked her as she stirred a pot of rice on the stove. "We'll arrange it later. It's in the first cupboard on the left in the dining room."

Her friend went into the dining room and looked in the first cupboard—no china, just a few chipped cups and plates. She looked in the second cupboard—no china. And in the third cupboard—no china. She returned to the kitchen. "Where did you say it was?"

"In the first cupboard."

She looked again—no china, so she wandered back into the kitchen. "Sorry, Elaine. I can't find it."

Elaine looked at her, perplexed, went into the dining room, opened the first cupboard, and started bringing out the chipped pottery cups and plates. "This is my china," she said.

"But these are all chipped!" her friend responded.

"Oh, they'll be just fine," said Elaine. "I figure that if people come to the jungle, they should be ready to accept what we have."

* * *

Marriage to a man like Cameron had come with many adjustments and Elaine's own independence and strong personality were redirected to run her home and support the work of Wycliffe. Cameron was an energetic visionary who exhausted many people in his wake with a constant stream of ideas and instructions. She recognized Cameron's calling to pioneer this era and lead missionary efforts to reach all nations with the Word of God in their language. She saw it as the noblest use of her own unique talents to work alongside him in that mission, by keeping their home running and raising their children to see the work of the gospel as beautiful and worthy.

Lima and a Leper

It was still dark outside, but the jungle was beginning to stir and the orchestra of birds was tuning up as Elaine tiptoed from room to room, turning on lights and waking sleeping children. Their clothes were laid out at the foot of their beds—dresses and black patent leather shoes for all three girls. The children stumbled into their clothes, whispering to one another as excitement began to build. They were going to Lima!

Elaine herself was dressed in a pretty, floral dress, stockings, and three-inch heels. When she left for the mission field, she had packed a good deal of jewelry, which many thought was unnecessary, but which she put to good use. Each morning when she left her bedroom, she was dressed to entertain a president, if he happened to visit that day (which he very well might!).

At last, all three children, several suitcases, and Elaine and Cameron got out the door, drove to the airfield, and were loaded into the plane. They took a moment to pray for safety and that the weather over the Andes would be good so they could get through.

At Home Around the World

Eighteen thousand feet above sea level, they crossed the mountains, handing the two oxygen tubes around every few minutes.

Once in Lima, Cameron had meetings, and Elaine and the girls set about unpacking at the hotel. They all gathered for lunch with dignitaries and officials in a dining room of the royal Peruvian palace. The children were wide-eyed as they walked down soaring hallways with gilted ceilings and polished marble floors.

Cameron and Elaine knew that showing honor to their hosts in this country meant learning the local manners and they instilled these habits in their children from a young age. Quarrelling or rudeness reflected badly on the mission to which their entire family was committed. Even little Elainadel knew how to curtsy and give the proper Spanish greeting.

Lunch was a grand affair with several different courses, foods they didn't know the names of, and small cups of strong, sweet coffee to finish it off. When they weren't eating, the girls occupied themselves quietly in little games of their own, like finding mistakes in the hand embroidered tablecloth. Everyone had their fill, including six-year-old Grace, who had surreptitiously unbuttoned her skirt to make room for the wonderful meal.

Unfortunately, when the group stood up to leave, her skirt did not come along. Cameron glimpsed the mishap out of the corner of his eye and stifled a grin but kept right on talking and walking an ambassador right out of the room.

That evening, Grace settled down into the comfort of her bed, enjoying the warmth of her pajamas that her mother had hung over the heater so they were extra toasty. The incident today had been rather embarrassing, but it was over now, and perhaps tomorrow they would stop by a donut cart, or even go to tea at a fancy hotel in the city.

* * *

A year and a half after Joy entered the family, Elainadel (sometimes shortened to "Del") had joined the crew, then Billy four years after that.

When Billy was still a baby, the Townsends took a trip back to Lima, visiting friends, picking up supplies, and meeting with dignitaries. As their visit neared its end, Elaine prepared to return home with the four children while Cameron flew to the States for meetings. His departure would be a little later, so he helped his family pack up, took a taxi with them to the airport, and saw them safely on the plane that would take them back to Pucallpa.

The girls talked excitedly about seeing their friends and all the things they had to tell from their time in the city. In the air, they passed around the oxygen tubes but everyone felt a bit ill from turbulence. A few minutes later, the pilot yelled back that they would have to return to Lima. The rain clouds had turned stormy around the mountains and they could not cross.

At Home Around the World

Back in Lima, they waited for a few more hours before trying the trip again. The same thing happened. There was no way to contact Cameron, so Elaine made the best of it and spent the evening finding dinner for the girls and keeping their spirits cheerful by impromptu games. Finally, on the third try, they got across the mountains, but an unexpected storm front met them and they had to return to Lima once again. The girls were devastated, and baby Billy had been fussing constantly for the past few hours.

They spent that night in Lima and were able to successfully cross the next morning, but Elaine was exhausted, physically and emotionally. Managing all the girls, keeping Billy fed and changed, and handling the luggage was enough to exhaust anyone. They were home, but the day wasn't over yet.

"Mama! I'm thirsty!" Joy complained. "Is there something to eat at home?"

Grace interrupted her, "May I read my book when we get inside? You got it off the airplane, right Mom?"

Then Elaine caught sight of someone standing near the house—a shriveled up old lady, slightly heavy, with dark hair straggling down around her shoulders. She walked with a stoop as one accustomed to hard work. Elaine's eyes caught on her hands—they were thick and knobbly with irritated pink spots dotting the skin; some had already turned an ashy white. Leprosy.[1]

---

[1］ Leprosy is a disease which affects the nerves, causes blindness, and turns the skin to an ashy white. It used to be fatal but can now be treated.

Elaine Townsend

"Do you need directions to the clinic?" Elaine asked, a little startled.

"Are you Señora Townsend?" the woman responded in Spanish.

"Yes."

"I haven't come for the clinic. I've come to ask if you can teach me to read."

Billy was starting to cry, and the girls clambered for first place in the hammock.

What was she to do? Elaine tried not to think about the many tasks awaiting her in the house: the piles of letters to read, piles of letters to answer, piles of suitcases to unpack, her own hot, hungry, and tired children. Then she stopped herself short—what was she thinking? She could get sick! Grace, Joy, Elainadel and Billy could get sick.

The answer formed itself in her mind: I'm so sorry, I can't give you an answer right now. Could you come back tomorrow?

Then she remembered the three small children who had awaited her in Mexico years before—and the lesson she had learned then that God could bring fruit from something she thought was insignificant, small, not worth her time. If this was from Him, then He could also protect her and her family from sickness if it was His will.

"Come inside," she told Marta. "I need to feed the baby, then we can sit down for a few minutes and start a lesson."

At Home Around the World

Three times a week in the coming months, except when tropical storms rolled through, Doña Marta paddled across the lake by canoe to the Townsends' home, where she and Elaine sat at the dining room table overlooking the lake and sounded out letters, words, and simple sentences. Afterward one of the girls wiped off the plastic tablecloth and set plates for a meal.

When a famous Peruvian educator arrived at the house, Elaine thought about postponing the lesson, but decided against it. What Marta prayed that day brought tears to the eyes of all who heard: "Lord, I can't thank you enough for having Mrs. Townsend lay aside her home and guests for me in order that I might know you more. I just lived like an animal before she came. Nobody cared if I lived or died."

In three months, Doña Marta was reading, although her failing eyes made it difficult. Elaine bought her a large print Bible and a magnifying glass, and for hours she sat and read by candlelight. What she found in the Word began to change her. Not only did she come to know the redeeming glory of the gospel, but it bore fruit. On their way through the New Testament, she and Elaine came to the command "Love your enemies, do good to those who hate you." Marta stopped.

"Is it God saying that?"

"Yes."

"How can I do that?"

"What are you thinking about, Doña Marta?"

"Since I've become a Christian, my neighbors are jealous that I'm not afraid of the evil spirits. When I go out at night to meetings, they put their animals in my garden to dig up my carrots and lettuce and produce. When I come back and see this, I open up the gates and let my animals eat their food. But God said, 'Do good to your enemies,' so I can't do that anymore."

From then on, revenge cycles ended with Marta. Her simple faith taught Elaine many lessons. When God spoke, she obeyed. When sickness brought her low for months and nearly took her life, though she was too weak to read, she found comfort in repeating Psalm 23 from memory.

* * *

On one visit, Marta brought a friend who had recently become a Christian, along with her five children. Another week, some company from Lima was staying at the Townsends' house when Doña Marta arrived for her lesson. As their company prepared to leave, limited space on the airplane taking them back forced one woman to wait behind. Marta began to engage her in conversation and it wasn't long before she began to tell her all about how God had saved her from darkness.

She had been a vile woman, smoking constantly, drinking heavily, and living like an animal. She was hopeless and desperate. Someone suggested that she visit the linguists on the base at Pucallpa, and there one of the nurses at the clinic led this leper to the Lord. When Marta expressed a desire to read, the nurse told her that Mrs. Townsend would be returning any day from Lima and would be glad to teach her. Two days later, Elaine had walked up to the gate carrying Billy and a suitcase, with three girls in tow asking a cascade of questions.

Some months later, as she and Cameron got ready for bed, Elaine pulled off her shoe and stopped still.

Quietly she said, "Cameron, come over here."

One look at her toe and he wanted to call the doctor. But it was Saturday, when the doctor took a break from his regular responsibilities.

"The doctor needs his rest too, let's wait till Monday," Elaine urged.

Cameron consented, though the sight of his wife's white, porous toe alarmed him. The disease, whatever it was, seemed to be spreading quickly. A list ran through their minds of all the jungle diseases it could be. Neither said what they were thinking, but they prayed over it together, then went to sleep.

During the Sunday morning rush of hair-brushing, shoe-finding, and record oatmeal-eating—all to the tune of chipper tropical birds and screaming monkeys—Elaine saw a group passing by on the path in front of their house. Again, she called Cameron over.

It was Doña Marta, with a group of her grandchildren walking along beside and running on ahead. "For that sight, this all will have been worth it," she said, "even if I do have leprosy."

On Monday, when Elaine got out of bed, the toe had returned to its normal state. It would be years before her own children learned of the incident.

Doña Marta promised to pray for Elaine every day, and she remained true to her word. Through her life, Elaine counted the prayers of this humble Mestizo woman among the greatest treasures given her by a good God.

But Elaine was not the only one for whom Doña Marta came before the throne. She prayed that all her own descendants would come to know the captivating love which had found her. God answered this bold faith as children, grandchildren, and great grandchildren (now numbering more than a hundred) were drawn into the family of God, including some who had mocked her faith. Several also became missionaries.

Her namesake granddaughter said years later, "She had a huge love for everybody—always with her arms wide open to receive you. She was always quoting Scripture, because Elaine helped her learn Psalms."

* * *

Lelia Morote was another Indian woman who came from a staunchly Catholic family in Cuzco[2], and the wife of a prominent Peruvian educator. One day, as Elaine prepared to take her siesta[3] after lunch, she felt the Lord prompting her to invite Lelia over.

---

2. Cuzco is a town several hours away from Pucallpa which was the capital of the Incan empire until the 16th century Spanish conquest.
3. In tropical climates where stifling, humid heat reaches its peak at noon, it is not uncommon for many to take a short nap after lunch.

"Surely you don't want me to go now! It's hot out there. I'll do it at three o'clock, Lord," she replied (apparently not remembering how that kind of exchange usually ended). Sleep would not come. She could not rest till she had taken her umbrella and walked the mile to Lelia's house, where she tapped on the door and invited her for tea that same day. Lelia accepted.

Unlike Elaine in her twenties, Lelia had not lived a good life. As Elaine began to share the gospel, Lelia expressed a desire to clean up her life so she could accept the good news and be saved. "No! That's the beauty of it!" Elaine exclaimed, remembering her own struggle to earn her way to heaven. "You don't have to be good before you can come to Jesus. He wants you before you're clean because He's the one who makes you clean."

Lelia's face began to change and a bright smile spread across her face as the truth began to sink in. The next day she returned, bringing Anna, her Quechua maid—something unusual for such a high-ranking lady to do. Anna, too, came to know the Lord. As they continued to meet, Elaine mentored Lelia to better understand the Word of God. Lelia drank it up eagerly.

"The Lord is making His promise in Isaiah 58:10 very precious to me these days," Elaine wrote to Cameron. "It says, 'If you pour yourself out for the hungry and satisfy the desire of the afflicted, then shall your light rise in the darkness and your gloom be as the noonday.'

Isn't that a wonderful promise? I don't know when I've seen a hungrier soul than Lelia. She is hiding the Word in her heart as fast as she knows how."

Meanwhile, Lelia's husband began to notice a difference at home. Someone sitting next to him on a flight overheard him describe an unaccountable difference in his wife: "I don't know what happened at Mrs. Townsend's house but there's been a most wonderful change. She's more beautiful—just radiant—but not only that, she's a better wife, a better mother, a better housekeeper. In every way, whatever this is has changed her life so completely."

The Morotes later moved to China, where Lelia continued to follow the Lord.

Jungle Adventures

The growing work of Wycliffe meant that Cameron traveled extensively, often being gone for months at a time. Elaine cheered and encouraged him by her letters and news of home while he was away. Often, in the age before email and text messages, she had to guess where he would be to address letters to the right country. Yet their marriage grew sweeter even through the absences. Cameron's confidence in her was evident to anyone who knew him, and Elaine provided a safe place for him to dream and to pursue the opportunities before him. If no one else believed his crazy ideas, he knew Elaine would.

If Elaine had a skill for hosting, Cameron had a talent for picking up extra dinner guests at a moment's notice. One April, seventeen guests stayed the night, but a tropical storm rolled in the next morning, extending their stay another day and night. Elaine always kept something on hand that she could pull out for guests at a moment's notice. She kept things simple and made a point of graciously encouraging her guests to help with whatever needed to be done. When the British Ambassador walked into the kitchen while they were making cookies, she handed him a spoon and invited him to join in on the fun.

Elaine made everything a bit of a party. If it was raining particularly hard, Elaine would borrow the mission's yellow jeep to drive her crew to school and they all felt as if they were riding a chariot. They took time for tickle parties before bed and long hours of reading while the jungle rain beat down on the tin roof so they could hardly hear the words.

For one of Billy's birthdays, an alligator hunt was organized by an Indian Chief, Tariri, for Billy and several friends. It was cold out, and apparently the alligators thought so too, because they only caught one about thirty feet long (a disappointment to everyone). They returned home to cake, ice cream, and hot chocolate.

At Christmas, Elaine would wrap up a few new presents for the children, along with some of their old toys which they had forgotten about. They paid her back in their own way by going through her drawers and wrapping up the prettiest things they found for her birthday. When any of the children was sick, Elaine would make a special meal tray and if Cameron was home he would pick an exotic flower bouquet to add. The children would pick flowers and stick them on the tips of the cactus in their front yard. Swimming in the lake was a daily activity, despite the parasites and piranhas abounding in its waters.

Elaine Townsend

During one period of a few months, boa constrictors were all the rage with the children of the base—Townsends included. The snakes were easily caught and could be kept alive with regular installments of mice. When the snakes began to appear in school, the teacher put her foot down. "Ok kids, you can bring your boas to school but they must be kept in your desks! You may take them out at recess." So into the desks they went to be peeked at and affectionately fed from time to time when the teacher wasn't looking.

One morning, however, the Townsend pet boa mysteriously disappeared. It had bitten Cameron.

* * *

Cameron's lifelong love of the ocean drew the family to the rural coastal villages of Peru during their rare times of vacation. Once, while running over sand dunes and exploring heaps of ancient ruins, the children unearthed a skull which looked like it might be hundreds of years old. For some unknown reason, Cameron and Elaine allowed them to take it home, but Elaine herself, in a relapse of her prankster self from younger days, thoughtfully placed it on the pillow of a childhood friend who happened to be visiting from Chicago. The resulting scream from the bedroom was most satisfying.

After having served its purpose, the skull was dropped by one of the girls down the garbage chute which ran outside the house to be collected daily. The next morning, while the children were at school, Pepe came with his wheelbarrow and, as the trash tumbled out, he spied something carefully wrapped up. He poked around with a stick and picked up the object, but nearly dropped it when he saw what it was.

A little while later, the police came knocking at the Townsends' door. In the end, they were persuaded that the skull was not of recent origin, but only after some fearful moments in which Elaine genuinely feared that she might be thrown in jail.

Elaine learned to treat ancient skulls and other unexpected things as commonplace. Every day seemed to be a never-ending string of unplanned, unpredictable events. Elaine's many responsibilities overwhelmed her, and she was tempted to neglect her time with the Lord. Many days were tiring, and the pressure of ministry was great. Company dropped in and out of their home continually and, as Cameron's wife, Elaine was the hostess to whoever came by—whether diplomat or Indian boy.

One of their furloughs[1] brought them to Elaine's home church in Chicago where she had become a believer, at Virginia Latham's class. Lance Latham, her old pastor, called her up to the front of the church: "Elaine, come share about your work in Peru!"

But she sat rooted to her seat, managing only to whisper urgently to Cameron, "Can you go up? I don't have anything to say!"

---

1. Breaks from an extended period of ministry which often last for a few weeks, months, or even a year.

It was then she realized that her spiritual energy had been dried up, and she committed to filling her soul with the Word of Life by setting aside time every day to read and pray. If she did not have this time in the presence of God, she knew she couldn't survive. Slowly, she learned to walk through the busyness of each day with joy and contentment.

Wycliffe itself had been started with the belief that every man and woman needed to have the Bible in their heart language (the language they first learned). Now, it was the same Book which sustained Elaine during Cameron's weeks away. The Word for which they expended their lives renewed their strength. Cameron and Elaine, along with the other missionaries, trusted God for great things and relied on Him to provide the strength they needed to do His work.

"'God's Word will not return to Him void,'" Cameron once said. "We stake everything on its power in the lives of those who feed upon it … The greatest missionary is the Bible in the mother tongue. It never needs a furlough and is never considered a foreigner."[2]

As they woke up early in the morning and wandered into the kitchen, eyes still bleary from sleep, Elaine's children saw their mother reading, writing notes, and studying the words of life, gaining strength for the day. Later in the morning, she led a Bible study with them all together. She made up games and songs to help her children remember and

---

2. James and Marti Hefley, *Uncle Cam*, 182.

think about Scripture. She would say a verse wrongly to find out if they were paying attention and to help them understand it better.

"Children, obey your parents if you feel like it," she would "quote."

"Oh, Mother, it doesn't say that!" Billy blurted out.

"Oh, it doesn't? What does it say?"

Billy looked at Elainadel, and they both shrugged their shoulders.

"If it just says 'Obey your parents in the Lord', without any condition, that means always, no matter if we feel like it or not", Elaine explained.

Among the busy days, Cameron and Elaine taught their children to enjoy creative work and to take pleasure in the necessary tasks of each day. Even young Billy joined in the enthusiasm when he decided to begin practicing his trumpet at 6.30 in the morning.

Elaine was determined in her creativity and cheerfulness. When dinner at a friend's house made her sick, she shrugged it off: "Oh well, I'll be better by tomorrow." Even traveling with three children in cloth diapers didn't intimidate her. When they got to their motel each night she would wash the diapers out in the sink and hang them in the car windows to dry the next morning. If it got hot they'd roll down the windows and away the diapers would go!

One morning, as they were packing up to leave a lovely cabin beside a lake, Elaine glanced around at her children, tending to their needs and aware that a fun vacation was coming to an end. They loaded up the last bags and, as Grace settled into a corner of the back seat, she sighed: "Finally I feel at home. We're on the road again!"

As representatives of Wycliffe, much of their time back in the States was spent fundraising and driving from state to state. The family stayed in dozens of different places while the children were growing up. Elaine always brought along some piece of home and passed the time on the road by singing songs and playing games.

Wherever she was, Elaine's natural talent for teaching was always put to good use. Each year, the Yarinacocha base hosted a training camp for indigenous teachers, selected for their skill and aptitude. Elaine taught these teachers, working through translators to communicate with them as she helped them develop and refine their methods. During one of these training camps at the Pucallpa, the Bible was being taught in seventeen different languages.

Once a week, Elaine organized "Literacy Nights" where indigenous people and missionaries gathered to visit with one another and play games. Elaine's endless imagination thought up activities that didn't require a shared language, but helped everyone get to know each other, like dropping a peanut from their noses into a jar, carrying cotton balls across the room on a spoon, and memory games—at which the indigenous people almost always won.

As indigenous people came to know the Lord, they became eager to learn how to read so they could read the Bible for themselves. This factor was one of the main reasons why entire tribes among whom missionaries lived became literate: they wanted the Word of God in their heart language. As they read and ingested its truth, the gospel brought changes in every area. Villages which had once been unsanitary and filled with drunks became cleaner. Flowers appeared, gardens were planted, children were better cared for, and education grew in value. New Christians started to realize that the Bible impacted their everyday lives, and it showed. Their faith began to bear fruit.

The Peruvian government also commissioned Elaine to create primers for their literacy campaigns in remote tribes. It was a monumental task, but one for which her decades of experience in education had prepared her well. The intelligence of the indigenous people was often noted, as well as their remarkable memories. When one little boy took home a prize for knowing five hundred different kinds of birds, his father exclaimed, "That's all you know? And you've been going to school? I can name a thousand!"

As they themselves served among the people of Peru, Cameron and Elaine saw their own children grow in a desire to share the good news and see others place their hope in Christ. Once when the family was on vacation, Joy noticed a little Peruvian girl about her age, also traveling with her family. She invited the girl to sit with her and began to explain the way of salvation.

Elaine Townsend

When Elaine began a Bible study for native women, the Townsend girls organized games in the front yard for their children. Then they began a "junior" Bible study, with a lesson, snacks, games, and songs—all organized by a rotation of the sisters. Leading this small group helped them to feel like they were personally involved in their parents' ministry. They would spend hours preparing for these lessons in Spanish, sometimes with excitement, sometimes nervously. The group grew to around twenty children and soon other missionary children on the base wanted to help. At least two children came to faith during these times, including Elsa, one of Doña Marta's granddaughters.

When an Indian teacher was flown to the base and bedridden for several months, the children made popsicles and Jell-O, and Elaine drove them over in the base's jeep to deliver the treats. They helped to clear the dishes when company came, often placing bets during the meal on whose cup of coffee would have the most sugar left at the bottom. They emptied their piggybanks to help pay for a plane to help missionary work in Bolivia. As teenagers, they were sent to visit missionary friends in other tribes and experience life in a remote area, which they saw as a grand adventure.

Although they were the children of Wycliffe's founder and president, Grace, Joy, Elainadel, and Billy were not treated with any special preference. It was only in adulthood that they saw the tremendous impact of their parents' work and realized that Cameron and

Elaine were known and respected by presidents and diplomats all around the world.

One afternoon, as a group of boys on the base sat in the humidity of a jungle afternoon watching an army of Leafcutter ants trooping across one of the dirt paths, they began to brag about their fathers. "My dad's a mechanic!" said the first.

"Mine is the radio operator!" piped up another.

A third was quick to interject: "Oh, that's nothing, my dad, he's a pilot!"

Poor Billy couldn't think of anything to say. His father only traveled and wrote a great many letters. Finally he blurted out, "Well, my dad's the oldest!"

In the midst of guests, traveling, and Cameron being absent much of the time, Elaine helped to create stability in her home. Later in adulthood, the children most often remembered the excitement and joy of their childhood in the remote and dangerous jungle, rather than the hardships. They took part in the life of the base with eagerness and abandon, and the strong, warmhearted dedication of the missionary men and women whom they called "uncles" and "aunts", whose children they ran and played with in the torrential downpours and piranha-infested lake waters, would stay with them for the rest of their lives.

The Next Frontier

After seventeen years in Peru, Cameron began working to establish a new mission base in Colombia and asked Elaine if she would be willing to move. The base at Yarinacocha had grown up alongside the children. Where there once had been solid jungle, now there stood shops, classrooms, a clinic, and sixty-eight homes.

To start over again in a new country with new people and nowhere to live was a daunting prospect, but Elaine made the decision to pursue joy even in this. They had to sell everything they owned since they couldn't take much with them. The children were told to choose one toy and a couple books—everything else had to be sold or given away. But somehow Elaine made it all seem like an adventure. They were leaving for a new life.

As they prepared to leave, Elaine received news that her sister, Shirley, had died in her sleep after an operation on her feet. With a heavy heart, Elaine returned to the base from Lima, dreading sharing the news with the children who adored their aunt Shirley.

At Home Around the World

In July of 1963, the Minister of Foreign Affairs in Peru, Vice Admiral Eduardo Llosa, decorated Cameron and Elaine with an award for distinguished service. A few weeks later, at a large gathering in Lima, the Townsends said goodbye to the missionary and Peruvian friends —the "family" they had gained over the years. The next day, Cameron and Elaine were decorated with another award: Peru's Palmas Magisteriales[1]—a prestigious educational decoration. In twenty years, Elaine had gone from being the supervisor of 300 Chicago schools to a nationally recognized literacy expert in the country of Peru. God indeed had marvelous and mysterious ways of working.

Three days later, the Townsend family departed by ship, arriving in Colombia on August 19th.

* * *

In Bogotá, the capital city of Colombia, the family moved into an apartment on the third story of the Wycliffe group house. Here, there seemed to be trials for everyone. Elaine's feet and back, still damaged from the crash, suffered greatly climbing up and down the stairs. Instead of the deep friendships forged among the women at Yarinacocha, she was now living with other missionary women and Colombians whom she hardly knew. She soon learned that even the women on her street did not know one another, so she set to work inviting strangers over

---

1. Teachers' Laurels.

for tea and making friends of them. She took the initiative to reach out, learn their names, and earn their trust.

In Peru, the Townsend children had known every person, tree and path. But here, there was not a tree in sight, and school was done by themselves in the stuffy apartment, by correspondence.

To make matters worse, there was terrorist activity in the city and more than once, bombs were heard going off at night. The windows shook and the morning papers were none too cheery.

The one bright spot was their pet ducks. Nobody knew how they managed it, but Grace, Joy, Billy, and Elainadel were frequently seen walking them around the streets securely attached to strings.

From Bogotá, they moved to Lomalinda, where Cameron was making plans for the new base. He had bought and restored a mobile home, then driven it down treacherous mountain roads to a lakeside spot which was already inhabited by several thousand mosquitos very happy indeed to meet their new neighbors.

Yet Elaine was undaunted and continued to invite people over and welcome whoever dropped in. She made a cheery home of that makeshift trailer and life continued on. Locals noted the perseverance of this veteran missionary and commented on her grace and nobility. She transformed impossible circumstances and welcomed in anyone who came to her door like a queen holding court.

At Home Around the World

Changes continued as Elaine's father, Herman, died back in Chicago and Lillie came to live with her daughter. Grace left to attend college in the States, and Joy too nearly a year later.

* * *

Around that time, the Townsends began preparing to leave for the States on furlough. Cameron was already traveling for work and would meet them there, leaving just Elainadel, Billy, and Elaine to make the trip. This would have been reasonably simple, but for the fact that the plane which normally flew from Lomalinda to Bogotá had broken down.

Elaine quickly arranged a ride from the base to town in "the Ox," as the missionaries had termed a large questionable truck. Another missionary and her four children, along with all their family's belongings were also coming along. So off they all went.

Once in town, Elaine found a bus to drive them to Bogotá, but after everyone was loaded up, the driver informed them that he *had* to haul a load of pigs instead (which would earn him more money). Undaunted, Elaine walked over to a five-ton truck sitting on the other side of the street and bargained with the driver.

Unfortunately, the truck was already fully loaded, but Elaine knew how to be persuasive, and soon all the children were climbing in on top of the load. Ahead of them were hours of driving over rough, rutted roads. Things could only get better. That was, until Billy threw up and made it even less pleasant. Six hours later it was dark, and they rolled into San Martin, only to find that the missionary guest house there was full. With no other options available, Elaine negotiated with another bus to pick them up—all the children, luggage, and two women—at the house.

When they reached the next town, it was midnight. As the bus slowed to a stop, Elaine stood up in the aisle: "Hello, everyone!" she said, addressing the passengers. "Would some of you gentlemen help us carry all these sleeping children inside the hotel?" Drowsy children were brought inside, and off went the bus.

Inside the room, Elaine got out a beautiful doily from her suitcase and laid it on the dresser, along with a few family pictures. For tonight, this was home. Tomorrow, the trip would be easier since they planned to catch a flight up to Bogotá.

But the next morning there was bad weather over the mountains and all flights were cancelled. Again, Elaine went to the bus terminal and negotiated for a bus to pick them up at the hotel.

During the day that followed, Elaine's back, excruciatingly painful from its merciless jolting the day before, became unbearable. As they approached a small town on their ascent up the mountain, Elaine made her way to the front of the bus and asked the driver if she could get out and walk for a few minutes. The bus slowed, the door opened, and out Elaine stepped onto the main street. She walked through that town ahead of that bus like a queen, greeting shopkeepers and pedestrians on every side, strolling like someone on a Sunday walk and enjoying that little town despite her pain. None of the other passengers complained as the driver came along slowly behind her and, as Elaine reached the end of the main street, she climbed aboard and off they went.

When, at long last, the travelers arrived at the group house on Calle 42 in Bogotá and were greeted by friends, someone asked, "How was your trip?"

"Oh, it was just wonderful!" replied Elaine without hesitation.

The Iron Curtain

Elaine woke with a start.

A glance at the clock showed the time was just after three in the morning. But that wasn't what had sharply pulled her from sleep. Someone was in their room. Thoughts raced through her head—interrogation ... arrest ... imprisonment. They were in Russia on the communist[1] side of the Iron Curtain[2], in a hotel directly across from the Kremlin.

How they got there was another of the grand adventures of Elaine's life.

Five years had passed since the move to Colombia. Lomalinda was still their official residence, but Cameron and Elaine had spent the previous summer along the shores of the Catawba River in North Carolina. Several

---

1. At its core, communism is the belief that there should be no personal property and everything should be publicly owned. This removes the reward for hard work and gives all authority to a few people in power who determine how to allot food, property, and other things of value. The Bible speaks very strongly against the principles of communism.
2. The Iron Curtain was a political boundary erected by the Soviet Union in an effort to maintain total control and to keep its people from all contact with the West and its principles of freedom

other changes had taken place: Grace had married, and she and Tom lived in Chicago; Joy and Elainadel were students at Colombia Bible College; and Bill was studying at Ben Lippen in Asheville.

Wherever they were, it was a hub of activity for their many friends, and Elaine was kept happily busy. By that fall, Cameron and Elaine had traveled to South America, Mexico, the United States, and Central America. It looked like "retirement" had begun for this energetic couple—a retirement filled with ongoing work for the Lord (and many dirty dishes).

But in the middle of these months, Elaine started to notice that something was on Cameron's mind. She knew the signs for this visionary! Sure enough, he stopped her one morning as she was carrying a load of laundry from the guesthouse.

"Sit down a minute, honey, I need to tell you something." He put his arm around her and they sat watching a cardinal on a nearby tree. Finally, Cameron said, "The Lord has put it upon my heart to take His Word to the USSR. There are over a hundred languages spoken by people who need the Bible in their language." He paused, giving her a moment to process.

What a crazy idea! It will never work! thought Elaine.

Then he finished, "If the Lord is leading me to go, would you be willing to go with me?"

She thought back to the day, fifteen years earlier, when she and Cameron had encouraged new Wycliffe missionary recruits in Norman, Oklahoma, to consider working in the USSR. The group made a circle and prayed that the Lord would lay it on the hearts of some to make advances in this area. No one volunteered, but the Townsends kept praying.

Now here was Cameron claiming they were the ones who should enter this forbidding land themselves. At eighty-six, Cameron had begun to show signs of aging and Elaine was already concerned about the toll his many travels and heavy responsibilities as the director were taking. It was no easy choice.

After a few seconds, she drew in a long breath and said to her husband, "If that's what God wants you to do, that's what I want you to do too. And if you are going to go, I will go with you."

* * *

In the coming days, doubts continued to come thick and fast. The USSR was heavily restricted. One did not just purchase a ticket and plan a visit. Every part of the trip had to be approved by Intourist, the official tour agency approved by the Soviet regime[3]. Many places were forbidden, since only impeccable areas could be seen by tourists—there was much to hide. It wasn't easy to get accurate news about the region since American and Soviet news channels were heavily biased.

---

3. The USSR was a socialist state which took personal freedom from citizens. The government claimed to serve all citizens, but its leaders grew strong and wealthy by taking from the people and the entire country grew impoverished.

After a wakeful night, Elaine wrote another entry beside her Father's promise in Isaiah 41:10, 13: "Mexico 1943, Peru 1946, Colombia 1963, Russia 1968." One more monumental transition remained to be bravely penned a few years later, but in every season the promise held true:

> Fear not, for I am with you;
> be not dismayed, for I am your God;
> I will strengthen you, I will help you,
> I will uphold you with my righteous right hand.
> For I, the LORD your God,
> hold your right hand;
> it is I who say to you, "Fear not,
> I am the one who helps you."

So it was that at just past fifty, Elaine found herself learning the difficult Russian language. She listened to Russian tapes while she drove an hour each way for language classes at Queen's University in Charlotte.

They moved back to Mexico that fall, and Lillie came to stay with them. Each day, a tutor came to teach Russian for an hour and a half. They recorded these lessons so they could listen to them again as they studied for another four or five hours that day. "It's lots of fun," Elaine wrote to a friend. While they learned Russian, Elaine's mother, aged seventy-seven, studied Spanish.

Amid language studies, a group of recruits began to arrive from Jungle Camp, and Elaine invited them all over in groups of sixteen so she and Cameron could get to know them. After spending Christmas in the

States with their children, the Townsends flew back to Mexico in January to continue their language study and to apply at the Soviet Embassy in Mexico for visas to the USSR, since the process would be easier there than in the States.

* * *

Cameron was gone one day when the phone began to ring. Elaine picked up the receiver: "Hello, this is Elaine Townsend."

"This is the Soviet Embassy. We have received word from Moscow that you can't come this year. Perhaps next."

Elaine put down the receiver with a sinking feeling. They had been working so hard on their language studies and now it all seemed for nothing. She shared the news with her mother and they both wondered how Cameron would take the news. He returned home tired from a long day and, before he had time to take off his coat and Stetson hat, Elaine told him.

"Praise the Lord, honey!" he exclaimed with a smile. "This is wonderful! Now we have our first no behind us!"

Most people would have stopped right there, but Cameron started to remind them of the many "nos" before Wycliffe was allowed to enter Colombia, and the setbacks before they started work in Indonesia.

Two weeks later, they were headed to the Soviet Union. Permission from the Embassy had come ten days before departure and Elaine had spent the entire day calling eighty-two people to alert them of their travel plans. She and Cameron realized that many challenges lay ahead for them and knew how essential prayer would be. Three days before their flight, Elaine wrote a letter to send to all their friends. She closed it with the words of 1 Corinthians 16:9: "For a wide door for effective work has opened to me, and there are many adversaries."

"We are not unmindful of the adversaries," she wrote, "but we are also conscious of the fact that with God all things are possible, and that prayer does change things, so please uphold us daily. Looking forward to telling you of many more miracles in the days to come!"

Elaine and Cameron had been invited to Moscow by the Academy of Sciences[4], which was perhaps the main reason they had been able to get visas at all. They were allowed to stay in one of Russia's most historic buildings: the Hotel National. Its imposing stonework exterior faced Lenin's tomb[5], and at night the two red stars on the Kremlin towers[6] shone right into their room. They were in the heart of the Soviet Empire.

Elaine had made their apartment quite cozy with pieces from countries they had previously called home.

---

4. An organization, founded nearly three hundred years ago, which is responsible for coordinating work across various scientific fields.
5. Vladimir Lenin was one of the most notorious communists and the head of Soviet Russia between 1917-1924.
6. Built 600 years ago, the Kremlin is a fortress which includes five palaces and four cathedrals. It sits on a hill overlooking the Moscow river and its white stonework and gold domes are striking.

Mexican scarves adorned the dresser, a fur rug lay on the couch, a Guatemalan weaving was spread over one of the chairs, and a family picture hung on the wall.

It was customary there for an older woman to sit at a desk on each floor of the hotel and monitor anyone who came or went. Shifts lasted for three whole days and nights. Of course, Cameron and Elaine befriended the women who monitored their floor, and some of them thought the Townsends' apartment was so wonderful that they brought other tourists to visit.

The first truly fearful episode in their travels came when an intruder broke into their room in the early hours of the morning. Cameron and Elaine had returned to the room quite late after a concert and had forgotten to lock the door when they went to bed.

As it turned out, the man was drunk and had entered their room by mistake. The monitor on their floor and a hotel employee came quickly to remove him, but the rest of the night was tense. Far more serious things had happened to other travelers and could easily happen to them, they knew.

* * *

During their search for a way to enter Russia, the Townsends had approached the Latin American branch of the Academy of Sciences in Moscow with the request to do linguistic research. When they arrived in the country, a Dr. Volski received them warmly, but skeptically. When they mentioned Wycliffe's film on their work in Mexico, however, he gathered a hundred and fifty of his employees for a viewing.

As the movie played, Dr. Volski was shocked to see that it was all about Bible translation and the vivid joy demonstrated by hundreds of people as they received the Word of God for the first time. It ended with the moving scene of women missionaries moving from the tribe where they had translated the Bible to another, where they would begin another translation of God's Word. Dr. Volski immediately dismissed everyone, including the Townsends, without comment. One Jewish linguist, however, stayed behind long enough to invite Cameron and Elaine to lunch.

A few days later they stood in her kitchen. While they talked together, she opened a can of sardines and Elaine cut cheese. She said to Cameron, "I understand that Christians pray. Do you pray?"

"Oh yes, Estella!" he responded quickly. "We wouldn't keep praying if God didn't hear and answer our prayers." He went on to tell stories of prayers that had been significantly answered in specific ways.

A few minutes later, Estella stopped him. "I want my husband and daughter to hear this. Could you come back tomorrow night for supper?"

The next evening, Michael and Marcia joined them. They learned that Michael was not only a member of the Academy of Sciences, but a professor at Moscow University and the author of twelve books on biochemistry and hundreds of articles.

Conversation moved to life after death and Marcia abruptly asked: "Have you been to college, Mrs. Townsend?"

"Yes."

"And you, Dr. Townsend?"

"Yes."

"And you mean to tell me you still believe in those fairy tales from the Bible?"

As they were leaving, Cameron offered his Russian New Testament to the Professor, who didn't act interested, but let him leave it anyway.

Little did Cameron and Elaine know as they left that evening that the story wasn't over.

* * *

Elaine later admitted that one of the greatest hardships during those first days in Russia was a telephone that never rang. She enjoyed the accustomed bustle of their family, company coming and going, and the many people who needed help and advice. Here, they were far away from all that and long distance calls to and from the States were expensive.

For hours, Elaine would sit at her "portable" Hermes typewriter drafting letters to friends and family. But even here, life wasn't all hard. Cameron took his wife to the famous Bolshoi Theater to see Verdi's opera, Aida, being performed. It was an exquisite performance. Another evening, the Mexican Ambassador and his family took them to see a stunning ballet performance—superb as only Russian ballet could be.

At Home Around the World

As an act of friendship, the Academy of Sciences sent a chauffeur to take Cameron and Elaine to the Gorky settlement in Leningrad, where Lenin had died. Elaine marveled at the beauty of the magical, newly-fallen snow. They dined in the home of a Soviet scientist, his wife, and sixteen-year-old daughter. Along with the rest of Leningrad, this family had suffered through the starvation of 1941-1943 in which hundreds of thousands had died. The Townsends gave them a Bible and they had a lively conversation until late that night, though in the end, the family said Christianity was not for them.

* * *

Early in their stay, the Townsends met a young Russian woman, Natalia, who agreed to give them Russian language lessons. They also made contacts with officials in preparation for survey trips into the small language groups of the Caucasus Mountains.

Cameron's primary goal during this trip was to develop relationships with Russia's skilled linguists so they could later work alongside SIL in the task of translating the Bible into more than a hundred and fifty languages in the Soviet Union. He was strategically forming relationships and learning as much as he could about linguistic work in this massive, complex region so one day the doors would open for missionary-linguists to bring the Bible to the languages of thousands of people.

One of their first real friendships in this country was with the Deshereev family. Both Yunus and

Elaine Townsend

Tamara were distinguished linguists and authors. Their younger daughter, Julia, was a university student and Svetlana had recently married and was the mother of two children. Whenever the Townsends were in Moscow, now and in years to come, they could be sure of a warm reception. The meal was always extravagant, and they knew the family had waited in line for hours to purchase many of the delicacies they so generously served.

During one of their visits, Julia became rather forthright. "Mrs. Townsend, do you know what the most popular book is among the students at Moscow University these days?"

"I have no idea! What is it?"

"The Bible," Julia replied, quietly.

Elaine was shocked and puzzled. "The Bible?! But how could that be when it is a forbidden book?"

"That's just it! That is why everyone wants to read it—to learn why it is forbidden."

"Where in the world do they get it? I know you can't buy it in any shops here."

"Some of our grandmothers still have copies," Julia explained. "We cut them apart and pass them around as fast as possible, always being careful that the faculty of the university doesn't hear about it."

Elaine couldn't help thinking of the large building they had seen in Leningrad—once a church but now a museum for atheism. She had read in their Spanish newspaper a plea for atheists to work harder because, despite all their efforts, including radio programs and compulsory classes at universities, the number of believers in Soviet Russia was growing. Even here, she knew, the Word of God could not be bound and it would never fail to accomplish its Author's purposes.

Always Winter, Never Christmas

That winter of 1968 descended on Moscow, but it was a winter without any Christmas. As a communist country, Russia rejected the Christian narrative of the birth of Jesus. As a result, Christmas was treated as a backward, ignorant fable to be cast aside by modern men and women.

But inside the Hotel National, Elaine brightened an apartment with Christmas music and set up a tiny tree on a suitcase. In the middle of a country preparing to struggle through the bleak days ahead, Cameron and Elaine unashamedly celebrated the joy of God come to earth. His birth was the very reason they were here in this cold and forbidding country. During this time, the words of Psalm 31:21 became precious to them: "Blessed be the Lord; for he has wondrously shown his steadfast love to me when I was in a besieged [strong] city."

That December, it was America, not the Soviet Union, that won the race to the moon. And because America won, Christmas was celebrated in space. As the crew of the space shuttle Apollo 8 circled the moon,

At Home Around the World

they made a TV broadcast back to earth—watched by millions including the Townsends in their apartment in Hotel National, Moscow.

The words of Genesis sounded out through the darkness of space to countries illumined in Christmas lights, and to countries who in their "progressiveness"[1] declined to celebrate: "In the beginning God created the heavens and the earth ... And God called the dry land Earth ... And from the crew of Apollo 8 we close with good night, good luck, a Merry Christmas—and God bless all of you, all of you on the good Earth."

That night, Elaine lay awake thinking of past Christmases with her children and her first Christmas as Mrs. Townsend in Pucallpa, expecting Grace. Cameron woke up and when he heard she couldn't sleep, they began recounting the years together and praising the Lord for each one.

As New Year's Day came, Cameron wrote a ministry update letter to seven hundred friends in South America and around the world. In the square outside their window, workmen erected a three-story New Year's tree, and snow began to fall as they strung it with lights.

* * *

In January 1969, the Townsends left on a three-month trip through the Caucasus Mountains of the USSR,

---

1. Soviet and communist philosophy claims that Christianity and everything connected with it is for the weak. They believe that modern science and technology have progressed to the point where people do not need God.

along the borders of Turkey and Iran, visiting educators and linguists along the way. This was the ancient home of civilizations founded before the coming of Christ—and of the 168 language groups which had presented such a challenge and opportunity to Cameron.

Russia could hardly have been more opposite from South America in climate or culture. Cameron and Elaine bought the local fur hats that let down on the sides to cover their ears, but even fur hats couldn't keep out the bitter cold. As they arrived at Baku, on the Caspian Sea, Elaine brought her typewriter into the bathroom where the tub was running a hot bath so her fingers would be warm enough to type.

This was a region with ancient history where artifacts from before the time of Christ and portions of the Koran were displayed in museums. In Sochi, they found a ping-pong table for rent at thirty cents an hour and Cameron, who seemed to have improved since their dating days, beat Elaine in seven out of nine games. Elaine herself beat two Russian men. What a sight it must have been—the wife of Wycliffe's founder squaring off against Soviet gentlemen!

In general, Cameron and Elaine found themselves impressed with the methods of the various linguists they met. Most had grammars, dictionaries, poetry, and, of course, works by Lenin and Marx—though they lacked any understanding of the Bible. Cameron was interviewed on several occasions for radio, TV, and newspapers, and numerous friendships began.

"Although most Soviets don't believe there is any life after death, yet in downtown Moscow you see huge banners across the street reading 'Lenin Lives Forever!'" Elaine observed.

Everywhere they went, the Townsends observed a strange contrast between the modern progress portrayed so enthusiastically by Soviet leadership and the media, and the severe shortages and poverty caused by the Soviet philosophy which had decimated the country and the fabric of ordinary life for millions. Though they recognized the spiritual effects of widespread atheism, it seemed that Cameron and Elaine did not fully understand the economic and societal damage caused by men such as Marx, Lenin, and Stalin, and at times believed the propaganda which was so energetically fed to tourists from the West in an attempt to keep up the image of a "progressive Russia". On the outside, everything seemed prosperous and glossy, but for those living under socialism, the picture was much different—their livelihoods were taken by the government and in return they received barely enough to live on (in some cases, not enough). As a result, living conditions outside certain areas kept up for appearances were squalid and dehumanizing.

During one of their long train rides to a remote location, an unfriendly man in a uniform came through and darkened all the windows, warning all the passengers sternly not to open the shades until they had reached their destination.

* * *

Upon their return to Moscow, Elaine phoned Estella, the Jewish linguist they had met six weeks earlier. She came over immediately and she was radiant. "You know that Book you left with us, Uncle Cam? My husband has read it all the way through. I have also, and two of our neighbors. We're happy now and pray to God every day. Could you get us some more copies?"

When her daughter, Marcia, married a few years later and had a little boy, Dr. Michael asked Cameron to dedicate his grandson to God.

Little did they know, as they returned to the United States from this first trip into the United Soviet Socialist Republic, that eleven more trips lay ahead.

Arrested!

Six months later, they were back in the USSR, this time with Billy. During their first trip, Billy (then fifteen) had been left behind at boarding school and it had not been an easy year for him. Now on the road, his junior year of high school would be carried out via correspondence courses. He was likely the only student mailing assignments from an address in the Soviet Union!

Last time the Townsends had taken eight New Testaments and everything had gone fine, so this time they took thirty. When a customs[1] official found four, he asked, "What do you plan to do with these? Do you have more?"

Cameron responded that they would give them to anyone who was interested, but this didn't impress the Russian officer, who only let the Townsends keep one copy. They promptly wrote to friends in the States, asking them to mail more. During one visit to a church

---

1. Customs monitors the goods brought into a country and prevents illegal import.

they had observed a man writing down every Scripture passage that was read during the service, likely because he didn't have a Bible of his own. They knew how much these copies of the Bible meant to starving believers.

In this land of strangers and religious doubt, both the Word and the friendship of other believers became increasingly precious. Through days of strenuous travel and intense interaction, they found strength in recalling the faithfulness of their great and powerful God who by his right arm had opened a way into this vast and formidable country. They took time each day to sing and read the Word and visited local evangelical churches wherever they found them.

* * *

About a week after their arrival, the three Townsends entered an area forbidden to ordinary tourists. Their time in socialist Europe had seemed reasonably safe up to this point, but that was about to change.

A group of linguists was hosting a banquet for the Townsends but Billy decided to wander around the town, taking a few pictures along the way. When he got to the village square he snapped a few shots of villagers washing their feet in a water trough, then turned around to find himself face to face with a stern policeman.

Taking pictures of anything that wasn't quite perfect was seen as a breach of the propaganda that the USSR worked hard to communicate to the outside world. Officials were trained to respond sternly to any kind of photography or writing which revealed life outside the small, groomed areas open to Western tourists. Billy was taken to the police station where his film was confiscated and he was given a long lecture in Russian which he didn't understand. Three hours went by and Cameron and Elaine, with no idea of their son's whereabouts, grew increasingly concerned.

The officials, apparently frustrated by Bill's lack of comprehension, finally came to the hotel where the Townsends were staying to borrow their interpreter. The Townsends had no idea what was happening until the interpreter came back with a very sobered Bill. No serious charges had been brought and the Townsends left the village without any serious repercussions, although they were a little shaken.

During their time in the USSR, all three of the Townsends felt a tension which was hard to describe. From Russia they flew to India to visit an SIL base and during the first evening there Billy exclaimed, "Oh, isn't it good to have this wonderful free feeling?"

From India, the Townsends traveled to Nepal, the Philippines, Papua New Guinea, Australia, and New Zealand. In a little valley in Kathmandu they attended a plane dedication ceremony[2], surrounded by the beautiful Himalayan mountains and Mount Everest. Cameron closed the ceremony by asking God's

---

2. Cameron had started the tradition of dedicating planes to God which had been given to JAARS in a formal ceremony with missionaries and officials from the host country.

protection over the plane, pilot and passengers in the years to come. In the next few minutes, the sun went down behind the snow-capped peaks, painting them all the colors of the rainbow. Elaine wrote that she had never seen anything so beautiful.

In Ukarumpa, Papua New Guinea, the Townsends were invited into the homes on the base so that they could get to know all 308 members. Each served their best, and Elaine bemoaned her growing waistline as a result.

Before they returned home, the Townsends hoped to stop in Vietnam, but hostilities with the USSR prevented this. Russian officials would frown on a Vietnamese stamp in their passports and might even forbid them from entering the country again.

* * *

After traveling sixteen out of nineteen months and visiting fifteen countries, it was no surprise that Cameron developed heart trouble. Yet he continued to rise early for prayer, remembering people around the world and their gospel ministry. Two decades younger, it took Elaine six weeks to fully recover from their extensive travels, but Cameron always seemed to bounce back nearly overnight.

The Townsend family was expanding and the next two years held many changes. Joy married David Tuggy, and shortly afterward they became SIL members, going on to do Bible translation in two different languages. Elainadel married Bob Garippa, who would become the Dean of Students at Dallas Theological Seminary.

Cam and Elaine celebrated their twenty-fifth wedding anniversary, and Cam his seventy-fifth birthday.

Cameron also resigned his post of General Director of Wycliffe Bible Translators, recognizing he could not continue to keep up with the many responsibilities. He continued working energetically, however, to publish a book on the success of bilingual education in the Caucasus: *They Found a Common Tongue.*

Elaine continued her extensive hospitality and took Russian classes. They put their newly-completed house which Elaine designed, right to work by inviting over sixty guests and hosting seventeen of them overnight.

* * *

In April of 1972 Cameron and Elaine returned to the USSR for seven weeks. From Russia, Cameron sent a telegram to President Richard Nixon describing one of the schools they had visited. As it happened, President Nixon himself was in Russia at the time for meetings with Brezhnev and other Soviet leaders. For the first time in history, the Grand Palace of the Kremlin carried the flying stars and stripes.

Cameron and Elaine took some time for rest as well during this visit, staying at one of the famous health resorts in that area known for its mineral hot springs. They took up ping-pong again and once more, Elaine took pride in winning against her Russian competition. This time it became a sort of second honeymoon for the two of them.

Cameron celebrated his 76th birthday back in Moscow and Elaine wrote to family, "He gets better all the time! We praise the Lord for the added strength provided for both of us." On that third trip, the Townsends were invited into twenty-nine homes—more than all the invitations extended to British embassy members combined.

Early in May of 1972, Harper & Row published Cameron's book, *They Found a Common Language*[3], and sent advance copies, which the Townsends took on their next trip to the Soviet Union that summer. Sharing this book helped forge new relationships and a respect for the work of SIL and Wycliffe, as well as its founder.

On one Sunday morning in Tashkent, Cameron and Elaine took a taxi to a secret address. As they drove up, they debated whether this was the right place—it looked like a big garage. Hesitantly, they started to open the door of the taxi when a young Russian girl walked up and said, "Yes, this is the house you are looking for."

They walked inside and heard Russian believers singing. It was an illegal church. At the end of the service, the pastor asked Cameron to say a few words, then they all sang *God Be With You Till We Meet Again* in Russian, some waving their scarfs and handkerchiefs.

As she looked around her, Elaine thought back to her friends at the North Side Gospel Center, and to the

---

3. A book about the role of bilingual education in strengthening a society.

Elaine Townsend

Mexican believers from the Mission in Chicago. In her mind she could see again the Aztec believers in Mexico, singing this same hymn as she and Cameron moved from Tetelcingo to Peru shortly after their marriage, and their beloved co-workers in Peru weeping as their family left to begin work in Colombia in 1963. How God had led all these years through hard and joyful times.

Opportunities for work in Russia continued to come. During their last week in Moscow, twenty-two people came to visit in their hotel room, including a newspaper reporter writing an article on Cam for the popular magazine, *Soviet Life*, and a radio announcer for *Radio Moscow* who taped an hour's interview. Professors from Lithuania and Ethiopia, students, and linguists came to say goodbye and Cameron and Elaine received expensive bouquets of flowers and other gifts. Elaine phoned to say goodbye to a journalist friend, and on the other end of the line woman exclaimed, "Oh, how I hate to see you go! You are the best friends I have had in this world. Please don't forget to pray for me and my daughter."

After traveling 60,000 miles that year, visiting the four republics of Turkmenia, Tajikistan, Uzbekistan and Kazakhstan, Cameron wrote at the end of a letter, "How could we retire when God gives energy and there are still 2,000 tribes without God's Word?"

Six days after returning home to Waxhaw, the Townsends received a call from the Pakistani Ambassador in Washington D.C.: the President of

Pakistan had issued an official request for SIL and Wycliffe to come do linguistic and translation work in his country.

A few months later, they stopped in Islamabad, Pakistan, en route to the Soviet Union. There they had an audience with President Zulfikar Ali Bhutto. Elaine and Cameron were ushered into the office of the President between two rows of tall, handsome soldiers standing at attention. For twenty minutes, President Bhutto listened attentively to Cameron's explanation of their language and education work, then promised to give land to Wycliffe for a base of operations.

After the audience, the Townsends were taken to visit a university under construction. Many of the educators they met there had attended Harvard, Berkeley, Oxford or other prestigious schools abroad. When they returned to the hotel, Elaine collapsed into bed for the next two and a half days.

"Friendship" the Trailer

The Townsends' sixth trip to Russia would prove epic. Cameron decided they could be more mobile and effective if they brought their own car and trailer (camper homes were very rare in Russia at the time). The only problem? There was no car, no trailer, and no way to get either one to Russia even if they had them.

Yet again, the Lord provided, and a few weeks later, they had both the car and the trailer. Elaine loved to drive, unlike Cameron, so she immediately set to work practicing driving, parking, and backing up the trailer. Bill agreed to come along as their mechanic for the trip.

The next job was to find a ship. The Russian steamer, *Mikhail Lermontov*, was scheduled to leave the New York port on June 12th. They booked tickets, and Elaine made sure to pack Scrabble for the long hours of sea travel.

Everything was falling into place. But six days before departure, they had still not received their visas. At the last minute, Cameron caught a plane to Washington D.C. to expedite the process if possible, but that meant Elaine and Bill would need to board the ship alone. Everyone at the JAARS base in Waxhaw gathered around them and prayed, then off they went!

Once safely onboard ship, the trailer quickly became an attraction. Cameron had painted "FRIENDSHIP" in Russian along the side, and Elaine had cut out beautiful botanical pictures from a magazine and used them to decorate the cabinets. She had also added cheery curtains, fresh potholders, and even wallpaper.

This was the first trailer camper to make such a journey to the USSR, and it was featured in several documentary films and newspaper interviews. The captain and many passengers toured it, and it was the topic of much conversation during the voyage.

Two weeks after leaving New York, the Townsends landed in Leningrad, but there they received terrible news. Somehow, their travel agency had not received approval for their trip from Intourist, which meant they must leave the country at once and wait in Finland to receive official permission to enter. They also learned that tourists to Moscow in the summertime were not allowed to stay for more than four days. Immediately, they went to the Lord in prayer.

Eventually, they received word that they would be allowed to go straight to Moscow as long as they promised to report to Intourist immediately upon arrival. There, they were given permission to stay for several weeks beyond the original four days. Increasingly, they became conscious of God's hand guiding this trip as He had all the previous ones.

* * *

The amount of driving they did over the next weeks was staggering: almost 4,000 miles over rough mountain roads, but gas was cheap and many people they met were welcoming. The steep mountain scenery through which they drove was breathtaking, with snow-capped mountains in the distance and herds of sheep and goats along the slopes. They forded streams with the trailer, hoping it wouldn't get stuck. A year and a half before, doctors had prohibited Cameron from driving even a few hours but now here they were!

In some towns, long lines of people waiting for their gas ration would let the Townsends go ahead when they learned they were Americans, saying, "You helped us in the war!"[1] Late one night they pulled into a village but couldn't find the place Intourist had scheduled for them to stay. Elaine found a policeman who led them to a gas station where he gave them fifteen free liters, then through all the red lights in town to their booked motel.

True to style, Elaine took every opportunity of showing hospitality to new friends in their makeshift home. During this trip, around three hundred people visited their "home on wheels", and the largest dinner party served eight. "A bit crowded to be sure!" Elaine commented, cheerfully. No matter how important or how humble, each guest found themselves graciously welcomed and served with whatever came to hand.

---

1. The United States and Russia were two of the main "Allied" powers against Axis forces during World War II.

Intourist then abruptly changed their schedule, requiring them to return to Moscow early. They drove more than ten hours a day for five days to get there on time. Through it all, Elaine wrote home, "We marvel at the extra strength the Lord is giving us."

Leaving the car and trailer in a guarded lot on the bank of the Moscow River to face a brutal Russian winter (not their brightest idea, as it turned out), Cameron, Elaine, and Billy set their faces toward the United States and home.

* * *

In the spring of the following year, the Townsends received word that their daughter and son-in-law, Joy and David Tuggy, had completed the first draft of the New Testament in the ancient Aztec language of Cakchiquel, which Cameron himself had begun decades earlier. God was giving them the joy of seeing seeds planted so long ago come to maturity and ripen.

Landing once again that June in Leningrad on the steamship *S.S. Lermontov*, Cameron, Elaine, and Bill made their way south by train to retrieve their car and trailer from the parking lot in Moscow. Getting there proved more of an adventure than anyone wanted.

During the passage across the Atlantic, Bill had said, "Let's pray that customs won't open any of our baggage this time!" Elaine was skeptical. Customs had opened their baggage on all eight visits. Every time they found a Bible in Cameron's coat pocket and inquired if they had any more, usually confiscating most of them.

Elaine Townsend

Now Bill wanted to pray that they wouldn't even look. Elaine mumbled a half-hearted prayer with him and went to sleep.

Arriving in Leningrad along with 700 other passengers, they saw a crowd of customs officials thoroughly checking all bags as usual. They moved through the line with their six new trailer tires, a car battery, and plenty of baggage. *Here it comes*, Elaine thought.

Suddenly, a young man approached Cameron. "Dr. Townsend? Is it you here again? Welcome to the USSR!"

Cameron looked at him, nudging Elaine with a frantic whisper, "Who is he? *Who is he?*" After a few seconds, Elaine remembered him as a campsite guard they had met the year before, with the addition of a new beard. The Townsends had invited him and his wife into their trailer for coffee and given them some printed portions of Scripture.

"Now, if you'll just wait a few minutes," the man was saying, "I'll take care of you."

He escorted them through customs and not one bag was opened.

They soon arrived at the train station, where they stored their baggage then left to get a hotel room for some rest before their departure on a midnight train. Around 10 pm, they came back to the station and asked the man at the Intourist office on the platform about getting their luggage out of storage. "You've got plenty of time, lots of time, just sit down and watch a TV program," he reassured them.

About an hour later, Cameron approached the counter again. "We have nineteen pieces of luggage to move out of storage. Shouldn't we get started on that?"

"I've told you. There's no rush," was the brusque reply.

The three Townsends became more anxious, until, at ten minutes to twelve, they heard the train warming up and Cameron again returned to the counter: "Don't you think we should start getting the luggage now?"

"Oh, you wanted to get on *that* train, didn't you?" At this point the Intourist assistant realized he had let too much time go by and a baggage man ran to get a cart, while three others helped load the bags. It was sheer panic.

The bag storage was at one end of the train and their compartments were in the first car at the other end, so they grabbed as many bags as they could and began to run the length of the train. Elaine had the tickets and passports, but she was several cars behind everyone else, struggling to keep up with her weak feet. Seeing it was hopeless, Elaine began to slow down, but Billy yelled back, "No, Mother! Keep running!" It was agony. The baggage assistants began to throw luggage on the train.

The next instant, the train began to move.

Elaine looked up to see Cameron jumping on the train and begging the conductor to stop. A vision flashed through Elaine's mind of Cameron stuck on the train alone, without any identification, somewhere in the middle of the Soviet Union.

But miraculously, the train slowed to a halt, with the conductor shouting "Quickly! *Quickly!*" All the Townsends and their luggage ended up on board somehow, except the tires, which they yelled to the hopefully remorseful baggage men on the platform to send on the next train.

As the train pulled away from the station, they began to catch their breath and look for their compartment. They walked through the narrow door, happy to finally settle in, when a man in pajamas jumped up from the lower berth.

Startled, Elaine said, "Sir, I think you must be in the wrong cabin!"

In frustrated English, he assured them he was not, and produced a ticket. He had come all the way from Bulgaria and, sure enough, he had a ticket for a bunk in their berth. There was nothing for it, so they squeezed in with this stranger and all their bags and spent a noisy, restless night.

The next morning, they arrived in Leningrad, where they met a man from Intourist and went to move their car and trailer while they waited for the tires to arrive on a later train. The vehicles seemed to be in good condition, but shortly after Bill started the car, something went wrong and a mechanic from the American Embassy spent three days restoring it to health.

It seemed like nothing could go right with the car on this trip. Entire days of repairs forced them to drive all night to arrive at their scheduled destinations. Heavy truck traffic had damaged the roads severely and there were many slow vehicles.

In the end, they had to leave the trailer behind due to continually breaking parts. They waited for approval from the inflexible Intourist agency for this significant change before leaving on the next three-week segment of their trip. Little did they know that one of the most remarkable experiences in all their trips to the Soviet Union was about to happen.

Driving with a dirty or damaged car was prohibited, so after each day of driving, Cameron and Billy would wash the car. It was on one such evening that a handsome Greek Orthodox priest walked up to them. In his black clothes and large cross and chain he looked striking. "You go … to Sochi?" he asked, haltingly.

"Sure!" Billy said. "That's where we're headed."

"May you … do you have ride?"

"Of course!" This time it was Cameron's turn to be enthusiastic. That evening as they sat down to dinner, they heard a knock at the door. It was Father Federenko, otherwise known as Victor. Would they also have room to bring his wife and little girl tomorrow?

The car was packed tight with six people and filled to the brim with lively conversation during the thirty-mile drive to Sochi the next day. Unfortunately, thirty miles turned into six hours at the garage. Victor and Cameron talked in the front seat, while Eugenia and Olga, her six-year-old daughter, visited with Elaine, read Scripture in Russian, and sang in the back seat.

Elaine taught Olga the 100th Psalm, much to the disgust of the mechanic who was working under the dashboard who could hear every word. At one point, he came around to the window and snarled, "You surely don't believe those fairy tales you are reading, do you?"

"Oh yes!" replied Elaine with her lovely smile. The more he made fun of them the louder they read and sang—here was a Russian mechanic with no choice but to "attend" this Bible study with lengthy readings from a forbidden book.

The next day was Cameron's birthday, and their new friends joined in the celebration. Eugenia offered Elaine a ring in exchange for her Bible, and would not be denied.

When the Federenkos learned that the Townsends' return trip several weeks later would take them through their own hometown of Kropotkin, they urged them to drop by for the weekend. "Come stay with us!" urged Victor.

Cameron looked at Elaine then explained, "We'd love to come stay, but as you know, Intourist sets our schedule and if we do not check in at our assigned lodging we will be given a large fine."

Eugenia wasn't discouraged: "That's okay. We'll pray that you can stop, and we're going to be prepared for you."

A few weeks later, Cameron had just handed over the wheel to Elaine when a warning light appeared on the car dash. They were just entering the city limits of Kropotkin.

"Do you think we could ignore it?" Elaine wondered out loud.

Everyone was tired after a long day of travel and discouraged by the prospect of yet more car trouble, but Bill, riding in the passenger seat said, "Mother, that could be serious. We should probably stop."

They hadn't seen anyone since entering the city, but as soon as the car slowed to a stop along the side of a city street a crowd of people appeared from nowhere and began asking questions all at once. A few minutes later, a policeman appeared and a dozen people gave him their versions all at once. He barked back that this was *his* job and *he* would take care of it. Everyone dispersed quietly. Turning to Elaine, the policeman growled in Russian, "Well lady, what do you propose to do?"

"I don't know, officer," she replied, giving him a bright smile. "What do you suggest?"

For a few minutes he pondered the predicament. They had no time to reach the next town where Intourist had scheduled their stay before the garage closed and, since it was Saturday afternoon, no one would be able to service the car till Monday. He turned back to Elaine, "Do you by any chance know anyone in this village?"

When the Townsends arrived at the Federenkos' home under police escort with an official request to put them up for the weekend, they found the Federenkos ready for their arrival as Eugenia had promised. Eugenia had invited a group of ladies from her church to help her prepare a meal for them. It was welcome after their long day of driving.

That night the Townsends visited the Federenkos' church, where they found nearly three hundred people gathered, but no chairs. When Elaine expressed hesitation because of her bad feet and back, the priest offered her a chair behind a screen.

The service lasted for three hours, with lengthy singing and a sprinkling of holy water. Elaine was saddened by the lack of real Bible teaching and the hopelessness of these people who used so many rituals to try to draw near to God.

The next evening, Victor's brother, a heavily-bearded young man who was studying to become a priest, joined them for dinner. Elaine gave him her last Russian Bible and prayed that his congregation would be taught more truth than the service they had just attended.

On Monday, the Townsends piled in the car to drive to the garage in the next town. But the red warning light did not come on.

Elaine thought of the three groups of people praying for them around the clock back in the States as well as Marta in Peru, and was reminded of the promise: "The steps of a good man are ordered by the LORD ..." (Psalm 37:23 KJV). She silently added to herself with a smile, "and also our *stops*, even when He uses a Soviet policeman."

Back in Moscow, the Townsends again worshiped with the underground Baptist church where people crowded in the aisles, on the stairs, and behind the altar, despite there being three services. It was a striking contrast to the Federenkos' Greek Orthodox church with its abundance of ceremony and solemnity. This church had planted fifteen more churches in the region since Cameron and Elaine had visited the year before.

As they prepared to return to the States, Cameron decided to give the car and trailer as a gift to the Academy of Sciences. One can't help but wonder if they had better success with the car than the Townsends had had over the past weeks!

"Better Than We Dreamed"

At home in North Carolina, Cameron and Elaine joined an African-American church, which was seen as a step outside social norms at the time. When they walked in for the first time, everyone turned to look at them, and the pastor stopped his sermon.

"I don't know who you are," he said at last, "but you're the first white people to ever step over that threshold."

Over the next few years, the Townsends faithfully served and loved this body of believers and Cameron occasionally preached.

On Cameron's 79th birthday, the final draft of the Cakchiquel New Testament was completed by Joy and David Tuggy. Elaine wrote to friends about how more than two thousand copies were sold or given away in just eight days: "What a thrill to think about the joys that await them as they too find our Savior and best Friend."

Since they were planning to make more trips to the Soviet Union, Elaine decided that a nine-week Russian immersion course in Vermont would help her master the Russian language and hopefully eliminate the need for an interpreter to travel with them. The camp was intense. Elaine was required to sign a pledge that she would not speak a word of English except over the phone and at the shop.

She quickly settled in, creating song sheets for a Russian Bible study she hosted on Friday nights in her dorm room, which she had made into a welcoming place. At nearly sixty, she persevered through the hardship of speaking a difficult language among total strangers away from home, family, and friends.

At the end of the camp, Elaine took three exams, each lasting several hours. Then it was over. "How often we are tempted to think that the success lies within us," she had written in one of her letters during these weeks away. "May I only give Him all the glory always."

* * *

Shortly before their eighth trip to Russia in the fall of 1975, Elaine's mother entered the hospital, but when Elaine called to say goodbye, she said, "Isn't it wonderful that I am here in the hospital and will have two weeks to pray for you while you're in Moscow?"

But after so much planning and working to form relationships, this trip to Russia proved to be one of the most discouraging. Some of their close friends in the Academy had been replaced by younger officials who were less favorable toward the work of SIL in their progressive, socialist country.

To make matters worse, Wycliffe was being removed from Colombia after the spread of false accusations and this information had reached the Russian government. Cameron and Elaine were called to a meeting where a stern man pulled out a folder and asked, "Do either of you know what was in the paper this week?" They looked at each other, then at him, shaking their heads. He then began to read troubling news about SIL's situation in Colombia. "So now we know that you are a part of the CIA[1], Dr. Townsend," he finished. "You are spies."

Cameron began to explain, but was stopped mid-sentence. "How could you possibly *not* be? You tell us you have 3,500 members. Who would support a work like this? It must be supported by the government."

It was useless to protest. To the Soviets, it was inconceivable that work so extensive could be carried out as a missionary endeavor for the love of a man named Jesus.

But Cameron and Elaine continued to start conversations and pursue opportunities. When invited to dinner with the head of the English Department of the University on Lenin Hills, they spent most of the three hours sharing the gospel with their hosts and fellow guests. They visited the Colombian, Pakistani, American, Peruvian, Mexican, and Australian Embassies, as well as the Academy of Sciences, and various homes.

---

1. America's Central Intelligence Agency, used for spy work internationally.

The Ambassador from Colombia invited them for dinner. After Russia, they flew to Pakistan, where the Ambassador received them warmly, then to Afghanistan.

In the lobby of their hotel in Kabul, Afghanistan, Cameron found a paper describing a linguistics seminar that week. Three years earlier, in Ashkhabad, Turkmenistan, he had met a linguist who was now the director of a prominent university. Cameron phoned him and he promptly invited them to attend the seminar. As the Townsends left the conference, a young man approached them. "Aren't you Uncle Cam Townsend?"

"Yes."

"Would you come downstairs with me a minute? I want to talk with you."

They went where they could be alone, then he told his story. He was from the Netherlands, but had taken an SIL course in England, and married a girl from Finland who had also taken the course. Currently, they were both at the Kabul University studying and seeking to open doors for translation with their fellow students. Just that week they had held a prayer time where they had specifically asked the Lord to bring Wycliffe workers to Afghanistan. Now here was the founder of Wycliffe!

This man wasn't even planning to attend the seminar, but God had brought him at just the right time. Cameron and Elaine invited him and his wife, along with two others, to their hotel room that night where they prayed that God would continue opening doors for the Bible to be brought to all the languages in this country.

Cameron and Elaine spent Thanksgiving Day of 1975 in the airport waiting for a flight to India. Relations between the two countries were hostile and due to a mistake on their visas they were told they would have to stay in Afghanistan for several months. At the last minute, however, they were allowed to leave, and they made it to New Delhi, where they had an audience with Indira Gandhi, the prime minister.

Indira, unfortunately, expressed no interest in bilingual education for India, and the ambassador there counselled Cameron to proceed slowly with the relationship. It seemed that India, too, had heard the rumors that SIL and Wycliffe were connected to the CIA.

Yet Elaine wrote in their New Year's letter, "As we begin another year, isn't it great to know we are on the winning side and that the things that are impossible with men are possible with God?"

Two weeks later, Cameron and Elaine flew to Bogotá, Colombia, to seek resolution on the rumors which were damaging their work internationally. There too, God worked powerfully to bring resolution.

* * *

On his 80th birthday, Cameron received forty-seven phone calls and 100 birthday cards or telegrams, including a telegram from President Gerald Ford. The mayor of Waxhaw, North Carolina declared July 9th

William Cameron Townsend Day, and three hundred people attended a celebration in his honor.

In a speech at the dedication of Wycliffe's Mexico-Cárdenas museum, Senator Carl Curtis from Nebraska stated, "Townsend and Wycliffe Bible Translators have done more for the countries where they have served than the sum total of all the [U.S.] government or foreign aid which has been extended to those nations."

Elaine expressed the heart of their vision across all the past decades when she wrote "... Our first New Testament was completed in 1951 and I just learned that now in 1977, seventy-one New Testaments are completed. Imagine the joy of the people speaking these languages as they can now come to know of the Savior who brings forgiveness, new life, and a hope beyond the grave!"

Despite the deep hope which animated her, this indomitable woman was often weary. "If I didn't know the Lord would give me strength for my day I could never make it," she wrote to one person.

It was on their ninth trip to the USSR that Wycliffe was finally given permission to send SIL linguists and missionaries to translate 1 John into several languages. It might have seemed like a small thing to some, but it was the result of decades of work and prayer.

Two weeks before the next trip, Cameron had gall bladder surgery, but the doctor wryly observed that Cameron would probably rest more on ship than at home (which was probably true). When they arrived in Leningrad once again, temperatures were cold and there was no heat in the city. They wore their coats in their hotel room but were still bitterly cold.

In October, Cameron and Elaine celebrated the sixty-first anniversary of Cameron entering Guatemala and ten years since their own entrance into Russia. Then, they hadn't known a soul; now they had many friends, and officials from the Academy of Sciences were becoming increasingly interested in partnering with the work of Wycliffe and SIL to translate the Bible into the many languages of the Soviet Union.

For four weeks, they traveled the USSR, then visited Germany for board meetings, and finished their trip in Washington D.C. where Cameron had an appointment with Ambassador Dobrynin of the Soviet Union. During the meeting, Dobrynin told them, "I was raised in a Christian home and I am one of you; a secret believer. My grandmother had a copy of the Scriptures."

Last Love

Nearly a year later, Cameron and Elaine arrived together in Moscow for the last time. For three weeks they visited linguists, scientists, and educators in Azerbaijan, Georgia, Armenia, and Uzbekistan, before returning to Moscow. They were zealous for the souls of this land to be saved.

At one Baptist church a lady asked them if they had a Russian Bible. When they gave one to her, her face lit up with joy. A short while later she came up to them and pressed an envelope into Elaine's hand containing forty-six dollars. To her, a simple, cheap Bible was worth every penny. This was God's Word in her own language!

On one chilly Russian evening, Cameron stepped outside for a short walk. Back in the hotel room, Elaine wrote one last letter home to the States on her typewriter: "... Many, many thanks for upholding us these five weeks. It has been far better than we dreamed, just as He promised."

At Home Around the World

* * *

A week after his 85th birthday, Cameron was diagnosed with leukemia. But that still didn't stop him. He and Elaine flew to Lima, Peru for the anniversary celebration of thirty-five years since SIL began work in that country. From there, they traveled to Bogotá to see the work there, then on to Mexico. Along the way they studied Ephesians together, meditating on the power of a God "who is able to do far more abundantly than all that we ask or think" (Ephesians 3:20).

After a Christmas at home in Waxhaw, Cameron was hospitalized in January of 1982 for acute leukemia and anemia. The doctor gave him less than six months to live. On February 3rd, he was able to return home and during that month, dozens of friends came to visit.

Years earlier, Elaine had been warned by those who thought the age difference of nearly two decades was too extreme. It was unwise, they said, she would be left caring for him in his old age. This had not fazed Elaine. She was a woman who loved to see the Lord give strength for impossible things, and this was no different. As the unbelievable energy of this leader began to wane, Elaine came alongside him more and more each day. She honored him in the presence of other people and prompted his remembrance of past experiences so his words began to flow and everyone around was encouraged and challenged by the wisdom of decades spent in the Lord's service. To those looking on, her care for Cameron wasn't a chore. It was simple: she loved him.

There continued to be much playfulness in their relationship, and friends would tell later of all the banter back and forth over dinner. Once, as Cameron laboriously ate his dinner (everyone else had long since finished theirs), he leaned over to a friend and said in confidential tones, "You know, Peter, Elaine just had another birthday. She's *much older* now," he winked. "So we're going to have to leave pretty soon so she can get her rest."

But Elaine could give it right back. On another occasion, someone had made a delicious tart and a fellow guest was humorously complaining about the small size of the pieces. "Oh here, have another one!" Elaine told him. "Cameron's trying to quit." So the guest got two, everyone else got one, and Cameron got none.

These two were devoted to each other and it was evident to everyone around them. Elaine was Cameron's lifelong helper in remote jungle homes, formal lunches with ambassadors, and in the last adventures of a long, full life.

This didn't mean Elaine didn't feel the strain of caring for an aging and sick husband, however, and there were times that her patience wore thin. She carried many burdens—unseen to all but the Christ to whom she tried to carry all her cares and sorrows. During sleepless nights she read Scripture and meditated on the promises of their faithful God who had carried them all these years.

Cameron and Elaine celebrated their 36th wedding anniversary on April 4th. These days, he was often heard saying, "God is *so* good to me!" He told one friend he felt he had one foot in heaven, though he told Elaine he was still hoping he could visit the USSR once more.

On April 23rd, at six o'clock in the evening, Cameron left his tired, well-used body behind in the hospital and entered the presence of the King for whom he had spent his life.

* * *

Nearly a thousand people came to Cameron's funeral and the time of sharing lasted for three hours. His gravestone read: "By love serve one another, finish the task, translate the Scriptures into every language."

Back at home with her well-worn Bible on her lap and a heavy heart, Elaine wrote once again beside the promise of Isaiah 41:10 which had held so true through the past eventful years—"Mexico, 1943; Peru, 1946; Colombia, 1963; Russia, 1968; *Widowhood, 1982.*"

A few months later, while waiting for a flight to Miami in the airport at Bogotá, Colombia, two Wycliffe missionaries caught sight of Misael Pastrana, the former president of Colombia, surrounded by six tall bodyguards. When they approached and introduced themselves, Misael immediately asked, "How is the widow of Uncle Cam?" Many others wondered the same thing.

A New Mission

After Cameron's death, Elaine's life slowed down to the pace of a crawl, and it was near torture for a woman so used to constant activity. In the forty years since she first left for Mexico, she had poured out all her energy and talents to support Cameron in the ministry of SIL and Wycliffe.

Now, after his passing, the vision to bring the Bible to hundreds of unreached tribes still burned brightly. But what was her place in this? It seemed no one truly *needed* her now.

One day, in the midst of these grey months, she woke up and made breakfast, then took down a well-loved Russian teacup from the shelf and poured herself a cup of tea. After time in the Word studying Philippians, she opened a small green notebook and started to write:

"Forgetting the past and looking forward to what lies ahead, I strain to reach the end of the race and receive the prize for which God is calling us up to heaven, because of what Jesus did for us" (Philippians 3:13-14).

At Home Around the World

May I not live in the past but expectantly look to the Lord for the future that He has planned for my life. I know it will be good for He has promised.

Getting up from the table she unwrapped three large corkboards she had bought a few days before. She thought back to the time, not long before his death, when she had asked Cameron what he thought she should do after he was gone. He had encouraged her to stay in touch with people around the world, helping and counselling them in their ministry work. These corkboards would be a start.

She set them on her dining room table, then began to pin on pictures of her family and missionaries she knew. The boards would hang in her hallway as reminders to pray for these men and women around the world.

After this was done, she got out her green notebook again and began to write a list of goals for ongoing ministry work: training new missionaries, encouraging missionaries' children at school in the States away from their families, recruiting new mission workers, making contact with women in government, ministering to singles and women, and spending time with younger children encouraging them to memorize the Word. At the top of this list, as a sort of summary, she wrote: "to be an encourager of the saints" (Hebrews 6:10).

She put down her pen and got up to refill her teacup. Standing in the kitchen she paused, recalling the many times she and Cameron had used these teacups when company came over. In that moment, the sorrow of his absence filled her once again, but also the comfort of Christ—the one who loves to comfort His children in all their sadness.

Instead of another cup of tea, she decided to go for a walk. It was almost lunchtime and there would certainly be someone she knew at the JAARS dining room. She put on her shoes, closed the door, and walked out into the bright summer sunshine. It was a new season of life, but Elaine Townsend was not about to retire and rest. No, there was too much to do!

* * *

The Tillet family had already explored a number of mission organizations, several of which expressed distress at their large number of children. They trailed along a crew of seven, all sixteen and under, that Monday morning as they toured the JAARS base—a hive of activity where the main operations happened, from mechanical work on planes, to communication with missionaries on the field, recruitment, and training events. At lunchtime, their lively bunch crowded around a cafeteria table. Everyone noticed them, but they knew no one. Suddenly, a woman at the next table said to Kevin, the husband, "I hear you're going to come serve with us!"

"Well, no ma'am," he replied. "I'm in the Navy, and I don't get out for another year, but we're praying and asking the Lord what might be next."

The woman looked around. "Are all these children yours?"

At Home Around the World

Their hearts fell. *Oh great, here it comes.* "Yes ma'am, we've been blessed with seven."

"I *love* big families!" she immediately returned. "Won't you come serve with us?" And with that, Elaine nearly won them over on the spot.

Upon Kevin's release from the military, the Tillet family trained in Georgia, then returned for another visit to the JAARS center in Georgia. "She remembered all the kids' first and middle names and had all their birthdays memorized," said Gale. "I don't even keep all *my* kids' birthdays straight, and I *had* them!! She was incredible for remembering people and things about them that were significant to her. That was why it was so hard to get her to talk about her story: she always wanted to hear *yours*."

As it happened, the Tillets had chosen the table next to Elaine's table where she ate lunch every day during the week. Absolutely anyone was welcome, and the more the merrier. Elaine would invite whoever she happened to catch sight of, then introduce everyone at the table. Whatever she included in her introduction, that was what she intended that person to talk about. Like Cameron had been, she was deeply perceptive, and strategized to help those people connect with who could impact their lives. Her friends all knew what she was doing and watched her do it with a mixture of amusement and admiration.

Elaine also hosted meals at her house, helping base workers and missionary recruits meet one another and form deeper friendships. At one point, she hosted luncheons three times a week for recruits, pilots, aircraft mechanics, radio men, maintenance men, and all their wives. She also invited groups of young women into her home, then drew them out in a purposeful way, asking their name, a little about them, how they came to Wycliffe, something God was doing in their lives, and lastly, a verse they were memorizing. Women left these gatherings feeling cared for and invested in the ministry, a small part of its heartbeat.

If you had met her, she would likely have turned to you and said, "Tell me all about yourself!" with one of her winning, inviting smiles. She was always fascinated by those around her. She learned how to ask questions to draw out even the quietest person and made whoever she was talking with feel valued and important. She could also remember everyone's name, even years later. No one could be around her without sensing the presence of Christ.

If anyone came to help Elaine as her strength declined, they could be sure that she would stop whatever she was doing to sit down for a cup of tea and find out how they were doing. "It was almost like she did not want to waste a single conversation—it should be valuable," recalled one woman.

She was slow to talk about herself and eager to hear others' stories, knowing that God had planned each conversation.

When asked once what she would say to young people, Elaine responded without hesitation, "Trust the Lord to take care of you." A few seconds later, she continued, "I've been with people who've gone to the top and they're not happy, and I've been with indigenous people who have nothing but Christ, and they're so very happy. Get your perspective right and He will guide you; He's certainly faithful. Listen carefully to what He's telling you, but take the next step, and the next step ... The joy of the Lord is our strength. We want to be enthusiastic Christians, don't we? Not just somehow, but *triumphantly*."

"Watch out, World!"

Elaine, of course, assumed that everyone else also saw "retirement" as the opportunity of a lifetime—or she was determined to change their minds. She quickly enlisted a retired couple who sailed as a hobby to take their boat to the Solomon Islands and serve other missionaries there. It was thrilling to her: she told them all about the story of the plane crash decades ago when Grace was a baby and about the beginning of JAARS, and soon she was calling this couple "the pioneers." Elaine wasn't too far wrong—boats would be the next avenue of development to reach much of the 10/40 window.[1]

Tom Hopkins had served for thirty years in the Air Force and found himself stationed at the Pentagon when Wycliffe dedicated the 200th translation of the New Testament in the Senate Office Building. After

---

[1]. "The 10/40 Window is the area of North Africa, the Middle East and Asia approximately between 10 degrees north and 40 degrees north latitude ... [and] is home to some of the largest unreached people groups in the world." (https://joshuaproject.net/resources/articles/10_40_window, accessed on 3/7/2021)

the ceremony, Elaine came right up to him. "Tom, I understand you're retiring from the Air Force tomorrow!"

"Yes Ma'am."

"Well, *Monday morning* you report for work with Wycliffe Bible Translators!'"

You didn't say no to Elaine! Tom gave her a snappy salute and drove to the Wycliffe office in Falls Church, Virginia that Monday.

"She was so single-minded she could recruit anyone for anything!" said his wife, Ann. "She was like Uncle Cam."

Just as her husband had done so skillfully, Elaine recognized unique potential in each person and saw it as her mission to fan it into flame.

***

Anyone driving down a certain stretch of road near Waxhaw, North Carolina during these years might have glimpsed Elaine walking from her home to the JAARS headquarters, a couple miles away. If offered a ride, she politely refused, committed to her daily exercise. People could have set their clocks by this routine, but what most did not know was how many people she lifted up in prayer during those walks; how they themselves were prayed for as they sped past and waved at Elaine Townsend.

Elaine loved to set goals and count things. Years earlier she had counted how many house guests they had at their home on the lake in Yarinacocha in a year. Now she faithfully logged three to five miles a day between her house and the JAARS center where she "hosted" her table in the dining room. She walked in rain or shine, often taking the uphill track for an extra challenge.

After lunch, Elaine left the dining hall and walked home for her nap. "We all knew what hours we could call Mom," said her daughter, Grace, "and boy, you did *not* call her at naptime! But then we didn't have a choice—she took the phone off the hook so it couldn't ring."

By this time, Elaine had nearly twenty grandchildren, and about a dozen great-grandchildren, ranging from babies to young adults. She loved being "communications central" for the family, calling regularly, remembering birthdays, and sharing news from other family members across the States or in other countries. Always the teacher, she found ways to make everyday activities into games for younger grandchildren. She helped them learn Bible verses, taught them to whistle and even showed a very young granddaughter how to do her makeup. As well as that she drove with a fifteen-year-old granddaughter who had just received her permit.

Not that driving with Elaine herself was a safe activity! There was the time she careened at breakneck speed down a street headed straight for a garbage truck until someone pointed it out to her. Swerving, she narrowly missed it, but insisted it had no right to be there and later admitted that it hadn't occurred to her to slow down or move since she knew she was in the right lane.

Elainadel remembered one trip to the States from Mexico when her mother had reached 100 miles per hour, but "she later felt convicted of breaking the law and asked God to forgive her."

When it finally became necessary for Elaine to stop driving, her car sat in the driveway for a time until she confided to a friend, "It is such a great temptation to get in that car and drive. I just can't have it here." So the car was taken away.

As she approached eighty, Jim Akovenko (then president of JAARS) became afraid she would fall, so he put in "Elaine's sidewalk" for her daily walk to lunch. Then, someone gave her an electric wheelchair. *Watch out, world!* Her children nearly had a heart attack from worrying about their mother behind the wheel again. "Who's she going to kill between her house and JAARS?!" exclaimed one of them. Fortunately for those concerned by her driving, Elaine could never get the hang of the steering mechanism so she never used it and they gave it to someone else.

* * *

Throughout her life, Elaine had been direct and to the point, and that didn't change now. Someone asked her to name something she had learned about herself and she responded with a smile, "I wish I could talk more slowly. But it's impossible!"

Cal Hibbard, Cameron's longtime secretary and close family friend often drove her where she needed to go now that she could no longer drive. On one occasion, she was talking—and fast. Cal's own hearing was deteriorating, and as they drove he had ask her to repeat herself several times.

Tempers frayed, but Elaine continued to rattle on quickly. Again, Cal asked, "Could you repeat that?"

"You need to get a hearing aid!" she snapped.

"Elaine! It's not my fault," he protested. "You just talk too fast!!"

"All right then, you do the talking!!" she returned, and silence ruled for the remainder of the drive.

Cal later apologized to her, she continued talking fast, and they returned to being friends. "It's true that she and I locked horns several times," admitted this dedicated friend of several decades, "but we always straightened it out just fine."

When one of Elaine's daughters felt the need to apologize to Uncle Cal for her mother's sometimes harsh responses, he affectionately reassured her: "Even at her worst your mother is not half bad!"

This woman was aging, but she was still Elaine—personality flaws and all!

"What drove Uncle Cam?" the interviewer asked. "What drives you?"

"What the Word has done for our own lives and how we couldn't live without it," Elaine replied without hesitation. "We want to share it with others, and the Lord has given me many opportunities now. Most of my work is with the fellow Christians who live at Waxhaw

... but I long to be where the fish are. I am very, very happy about every chance I get to be with people who are not Christians.

"People ask, 'Can't we travel with you?' because I'm getting older. Well," she continued with a twinkle in her eye, "I'm not *getting* older, I *am* older! They want to carry my baggage, but I really prefer to go by myself so I can make contacts with people who don't know the Lord. It's been wonderful, wonderful, wonderful to keep me alive. When you meditate on His love, and what He's done for us, it changes your life, doesn't it?"

However, as Elaine's strength declined, she did agree to traveling companions. Along with Peggy Richards, a good friend, Elaine set out on yet another trip around the world. For three months, she and Peggy visited Wycliffe bases to encourage field workers. She had lost none of her liveliness and, as Peggy remembered, "She'd find something fun to do everywhere."

In one remote village in Indonesia, Elaine decided to go for a walk. Jim Akovenko and his wife, Sue, had also come along, and he protested. But finally he gave in and Elaine got her way. When a long time had passed and Elaine did not return, they began to get worried. At last, a policeman walked in, bringing Elaine. She had fallen, but in her mind it was all okay. She had wanted to go on an adventure and that's what she'd done!

In Peru, she gathered with three hundred and fifty other Peruvians to celebrate fifty years since she and Cameron had entered this country. When she visited the base at Yarinacocha on the shores of the lake where she and Cameron and their children had spent so many happy years, she was greeted by a lovely Peruvian woman who now lived in the home which had once been the Townsend's. The woman embraced Elaine warmly, then told the story of how Elaine had led her to the Lord in that very home when she was twelve years old. Now she was the mother of six children, all of whom were following the Lord.

But for Elaine, the most deeply moving part of the visit took place in a remote area near the Yarina base. After more than thirty years, Doña Marta was now over a hundred years old. Elaine found her in the middle of the jungle perched next to a radio given her by one of the missionaries. Her nose had been eaten away by her leprosy and she had almost died a few weeks before, but here she was, and the two women spent a few happy hours remembering Marta's salvation, reciting their favorite passages of Scripture, and recalling the hymns they used to sing together.

Marta told Elaine that she had prayed for her every day since she left Peru. They prayed one final time and, as she turned to go, Elaine's eyes uncharacteristically filled with tears, knowing this was the last time she would see her dear friend on this earth.

Back in Waxhaw, Elaine was hosting a women's luncheon at her home when the phone rang. After a hundred and five years of life, Doña Marta was now in heaven.

At Home Around the World

* * *

Despite waning strength, Elaine still kept up on the work of Wycliffe around the world and always loved to hear the news from the field. If she heard news which Jim as the president hadn't even heard yet, she'd exclaim, "I gotcha!" with her usual playfulness.

She attended every board meeting, asking perceptive questions and thinking of things that no one else had. People around her slowly began to understand how integral a role she had played all along in the development of Wycliffe alongside her husband.

In 2000, as Wycliffe Russia prepared to dedicate a new office in St. Petersburg, Jim and Sue offered themselves as Elaine's traveling companions once again. And so it was that at eighty-five, Elaine returned to that land where she had traveled and worked and witnessed to the gospel over the span of eleven years.

During their travels, Elaine spoke at a new Christian university, several schools, and at the large Baptist congregation in town (formerly underground) whose fellowship she remembered so well. It was her first visit without Cameron and she faced new waves of sorrow, remembering hard and happy times together in years past. One of their stops included a hotel where she and Cameron had lived during one of their longer trips. "Oh, it's so different. I hardly recognize the place!" she exclaimed when she saw it. That night Elaine cried herself to sleep, overwhelmed by the memories.

For nine days, several Russian members of Wycliffe, including a certain man named Slava, acted as chauffeurs for the three travelers. Unfortunately for him, Slava's English wasn't wonderful, so Elaine became his schoolmaster, taking every opportunity to instruct him, and more than a few car rides turned into English drills for Slava.

* * *

April 1st dawned: the big day. As she struggled with her presentation, Elaine felt the Lord leading her to abandon the speaking notes she had prepared. What He laid on her heart that day, as she stood before the newly-formed board of Wycliffe Russia, was the vibrant tale of God's faithfulness that had provided for the ministry of Wycliffe during its infancy.

What Elaine didn't know was how discouraged these men were by the hard circumstances they faced in their work and how similar their situation was to that which Cameron had faced during the establishment of Wycliffe and SIL. She followed the Spirit's leading and spoke of the ways God had guided Cameron and her in their work over decades, radiating confidence and boldness. Her words encouraged them in a way few other things could have done and these men were encouraged to press forward, trusting God to provide. And He did.

In the margin next to Isaiah 41:10, Elaine wrote once more, *"All this way the Lord has led me. To Him be the glory."*

Unbeatable

People frequently asked Elaine if she didn't get tired sometimes. "Of course I do!" she responded. "But I'd get tired sitting in a rocking chair too, so I might as well be out doing what the Lord has asked me to do! I said *yes* to the Lord, and I have no regrets! At eighty-seven, life is still exciting, and I look forward to every day. I enjoy my work so much. I love to write letters. I love to telephone. I love to travel. I love to talk with people. I love to entertain. It doesn't seem like work anymore. It's just pure joy."

She challenged the missionaries who went to the field to "try it out." "It's about a commitment," she would say. "Go, and be willing to stay! Make it a life project. We did that fifty years ago, and a lot of us are still going strong ... We have to be available for anything the Lord wants us to do."

When asked if she had any regrets, she replied in her winning, transparent style, "No. Isn't that wonderful? It would be awful to come this close to death and regret what you've done. No, I don't have any regrets." Then she added, "Well, I could have been more cheerful."

"I think of that verse," she continued, "where Paul says, 'It is required of stewards that they be found faithful'—not successful, not popular, but *faithful*."[1]

From the first day when she understood grace in that Bible study at the North Side Gospel Center, Elaine had lived for God. She was described well as "the tireless keeper of the flame for her late husband's vision." Cameron had sacrificed everything for the sake of unreached people who didn't have the Bible in their language, and now Elaine had lived out her life for the same mission: seeing the living Word of God translated into every tongue on earth.

She could never have dreamed of all the fruit God would bring from her surrender—she simply sought to be obedient to Him each day and left the rest in His hands. Her gratitude for the free and overflowing grace of Christ knew no bounds. She never got over the love of Christ. He was beautiful to her, and she wanted everyone to know this Savior of hers. "For years I thought He was just a Judge marking my good days and bad days and maybe I had enough good days to make heaven," she said. "But it's not that way—He *loves* us! He loves *us*!"

* * *

The last years of Elaine's life held severe trials. She suffered a stroke that affected her speech, then she

---

[1] 1 Corinthians 4:2.

began to lose her sight. She had been an articulate, vibrant woman all her life, but now she was a prisoner inside a body that felt unfamiliar and unresponsive.

Losing her vision was the greatest trial of all, because it meant she could no longer read the Word. This had been her lifeline, and to not be able to study and read was nearly unbearable. She listened to it on tape and asked others to read, but it wasn't the same. Her heart was heavy and many days were dark with discouragement, but through the struggle of each day, she strove to see His love even in the trials He had allowed to touch her, and she offered herself yet again to her gentle Father.

Even on days when Elaine was struggling, people left her presence feeling as if they were the ones who were blessed. Esther, a young African woman from Cameroon, once came to visit Elaine, only to be told at the door that she was not taking visitors that evening. Elaine came up behind the person who had answered the door and said, "Oh, I'll see *her*!"

Esther said later, "She was dying graciously... reminding me of God's limitless power—that we serve a God who is amazingly awesome ... and we can't put Him in a box ..."

When she entered a nursing home she told all her friends she was excited to be around nonbelievers so she could tell them the good news of the gospel.

Even the maintenance men coming to her nursing home apartment did not escape untouched. Bearing hammers, screwdrivers, and other repair equipment, they were stopped partway through their job and asked by Elaine to say a verse. Then she asked for a hymn. They weren't sure if she was more pleased with their dubious singing or with just getting them to sing at all.

Even after her stroke, Elaine faithfully exercised every day, working hard to be able to walk again. Visitors would walk in to see her raising her arms and legs up and down, building strength. Through her pain, she still retained a bit of her original spark. One of her carers tried to keep her away from sugar, but when one of her children came to visit she beckoned them over: "Go get me a Milky Way!"

"Where are they, Mom?"

"They're under my underwear," she replied in a whisper.

* * *

As her sight continued to fade, Elaine continued to recognize dozens of people simply from the tone of their voices. Even from her hospital bed, she continued to "host" everyone who walked into her room, greeting them warmly with a bright smile.

After a second stroke, a deeper peace seemed to take hold of Elaine. As she drew near to her eternal home, her Heavenly Father granted his daughter a deeper longing for heaven and His presence. "Thank you, Jesus, that my homeland is in heaven where you are" she wrote in her journal. "I'm looking forward to your return—oh, so much!"

Elaine Townsend

As a sort of symbol of her life, nurses of four different nationalities cared for Elaine during her last days in the hospital. Peter, a friend who had previously traveled to Ghana came to visit her and while he stood by Elaine's bed, a Ghanaian nurse walked through the door. Peter asked, "I wonder if you would recognize this?" and began a song he had learned in Ghana, stomping his feet in a sort of rhythm.

The face of that nurse lit up in a heartbeat, his face came alive, and he joined Peter, singing in his own language, "God, in Christ Jesus, is *stamping* on the head of the Enemy" (a song based on Genesis 3:15 and the ultimate victory of Christ over Satan).

When they finished, the nurse exclaimed, "I have not heard my language since I left Africa!" As he described it later, Peter said, "I knew this moment was between the man from Ghana and Aunt Elaine—I just happened to get to see it. And that told me not how much Elaine Townsend loved God, *but how much God loved Elaine Townsend.*"

She entered into the presence of her sweet Master a few days later, on July 14th, 2007, with that victory song as one of the last things she witnessed on this earth. The cross had transformed her, and through her the lives of countless others.

Elaine Townsend Timeline

1914: The Panama Canal opens.

1915: Elaine Mielke born in Chicago.

1918: World War I ends on November 11th.

1927: Charles Lindbergh makes the first solo, nonstop transatlantic flight in the Spirit of St. Louis.

1933: Hitler becomes chancellor of Germany.

1936: Elaine leaves on her trip around the world.
Elaine becomes a Christian.

1939: Elaine starts teaching in Chicago.
Germany invades Poland, beginning World War II.

1941: Cameron calls SIL to pray for fifty new workers to double their team in the coming year.

1942: Elaine attends the Summer Institute of Linguistics.
Elaine is appointed school supervisor in Chicago.

1943: Elaine leaves for Mexico as a Wycliffe Missionary.

1945: Germany surrenders on May 7th and Japan on August 14th.
Cameron and Elaine become engaged (October).

1946: Cameron and Elaine are married on April 4th and move to Peru on April 20th.
Elaine conducts literacy campaigns in the Andes mountains.
Grace born in Lima.

1947: Cameron and Elaine are in a major plane crash.

1948: Joy is born in Mexico on Cinco de Mayo.

1949: Elainadel is born in Yarinacocha.

1953: Billy is born in Peru.

1958: America launches her first satellite, Explorer I.

1963: The Townsends move to Colombia.

1968: Cameron and Elaine visit the USSR on the first of eleven trips together.

1969: Neil Armstrong and Edwin Aldrin become the first men to walk on the moon.

1970: Cameron and Elaine move to Waxhaw, North Carolina.

1971: Cameron resigns as the General Director of Wycliffe Bible Translators.

1975: Elaine attends a nine-week intensive Russian course in Vermont.

1982: Cameron dies on April 23rd.

1983: The Internet begins.

2000: Elaine visits Russia for the last time.

2001: Hijackers fly passenger planes into the World Trade Center Towers in New York.

2005: Elaine attends her first Bible dedication.
Hurricane Katrina devastates New Orleans.

2007: Elaine meets Jesus on July 14th.

Thinking Further Topics

Chapter 1: Disaster!

Our lives can change in an instant. How should a Christian think differently about something scary than a person who doesn't believe God exists? Read Romans 8:13-39 and think about how these verses affect our view of hard things.

Chapter 2: Early Mischief

Write down a list of things you enjoy. How would you feel if they were all taken away from you? Elaine's early years helped teach her that happiness wasn't dependent on nice things. How can you grow in contentment with what you have?

Chapter 3: A Trip Around the World

Elaine's perspective on the world was broadened by visiting many unfamiliar places. What are the ways you are learning to understand the world better? Are there books you can read or people you can talk to about what it is like to live in another part of the world?

Chapter 4: A Shocking Realization

Have you ever explained to someone how they can be saved? Think about what Virginia taught Elaine about Christ's work for her. Write out two of the verses Elaine looked up on a small notecard and memorize them.

Chapter 5: Miss Mielke

Elaine said, "You never know what will happen when you say, 'Yes, Lord! Where you lead me, I will follow,' but I've never, ever heard a missionary say, 'Oh, I wish I hadn't followed the Lord. I made a big mistake.' To the contrary! No matter how sick they are and no matter what they've gone through, they're happy. So happy." Have you made a decision that had hard consequences but was worth it anyway? What do you think was the "better thing" for Elaine and the missionaries she knew?

Chapter 6: Budding Romance

Elaine took advantage of many opportunities to develop her gifts. She did not wait for a husband to come and find her. What skills do you have that God might use? Read Matthew 25:14-30 and consider what it means to be given something to steward.

Chapter 7: The Crash

What would life be like if you couldn't use your legs for six months? Do you think you would be discouraged, like Elaine? What helped Elaine change her perspective on the airplane crash? Can you trust God in the middle of hard times? Is there someone in your life who can help remind you of God's goodness?

Chapter 8: Lima and a Leper

Elaine had lots of good reasons why she could have decided not to help Doña Marta. Are there things keeping you back from helping others or telling them about Jesus? Do you know anyone who is good at loving other people? Is it always easy for them? Pray that God would show you opportunities to love people, especially those you find it hard to love.

Chapter 9: Jungle Adventures

What aspects of living in the jungle sound like fun? What parts sound scary or unpleasant? God gives us wonderful and hard things at the same time. Did Elaine honor God with the hard parts or the easy parts of living at Yarinacocha (or both)? Make a list of hard things in your life and things you love about your life. How do you think you can honor God with both lists?

Chapter 10: The Next Frontier

What do you think went through Elaine's mind when Cameron first asked about moving to Colombia? What would you have thought? Serving God where He called her to be was the most important thing to Elaine and she was willing to give up everything to be in the center of His will. Look up Proverbs 3:6. What does it mean to "trust in the Lord with all your heart"?

Chapter 11: The Iron Curtain

Sometimes the best things take the most perseverance. What things did Elaine encounter in trying to get to Russia that would have caused you to give up? Why do you think she and Cameron kept trying? What things in your life are worth doing that require perseverance?

Pray and ask God to give you the dedication and patience you need.

Chapter 12: Always Winter, Never Christmas

Cameron and Elaine learned much from the educators and linguists in the USSR. However, some of the good results happened as a result of government oppression. Do you think bad people can ever do good things? Read Matthew 5:45. On this earth, God shows mercy to good people and bad people in countless ways (like rain watering the crops of evil and good men). God sometimes enables bad people to do remarkable things. We can be grateful for the things they accomplish while also realizing that God is displeased by their sin.

Chapter 13: Arrested!

Elaine (and Cameron) made a lasting impression on people in countries that didn't trust the Bible. What was it about Elaine that was so attractive to those she met? Sometimes, unbelievers see the friendliness and the love of Christians and start to wonder why they are more joyful and caring. How does your life look different from people who don't believe in God? God has loved you by sending His Son to die for your sins. How can you be better at showing others that same love?

Chapter 14: "Friendship" the Trailer

If you were in Elaine's position, would you have been frustrated by the car continuing to break down, or excited to see what God would do even through this inconvenience? Do you think trusting God is a feeling or a choice? Why? If God commands us to trust Him (see Psalm 3:5-6), do you think He will help you to do that? Look up Philippians 4:19.

Chapter 15: "Better Than We Dreamed"

In their New Year's letter Elaine wrote, "May I share with you my verse for 1979? Colossians 2:7 (TLB): 'Let your roots grow down into him. See that you go on growing in the Lord, and become strong and vigorous in the truth you were taught. Let your lives overflow with joy and thanksgiving for all he has done.' Let's pray these goals for each other and then be able to look back over the days, weeks, and months, and see how He has enabled us to grow deeper in Him, to be stronger and more vigorous, more joyful and thankful." What helps you to grow stronger in your love for the Lord? Ask your parents or an older friend what encourages them in their walk with the Lord.

Chapter 16: Last Love

Do you know any married people who are loving their spouses through a difficult time? Even in hard times Elaine served Cameron joyfully. Was this easy or did she have to work at it? Think over the lessons God taught her—relying on His strength, loving others, walking in the center of His will. Isn't it amazing how God leads us gently and teaches us the lessons we need along the way?

Chapter 17: A New Mission

Even though she lacked the close friendships that might have encouraged her after Cameron's death, Elaine determined to show the love of Christ to people where she lived. It's often easier to hang out around people who like us and meet our needs. What opportunities do you have to reach out to people who others might forget? Look up John 15:12-13 and consider how God's love toward us affects our love for other people.

Chapter 18: "Watch Out, World!"

Do you know any elderly people who love the Lord and are serving others faithfully? Can you help them even in little ways? You may be surprised by how much you can encourage them—and also by how much fun they are and the amazing stories they have to tell!

Chapter 20: Unbeatable

One young woman who knew Elaine described her this way: "Elaine fundamentally identified herself as Christ's. She seemed to divide her life into two portions: 'pre-Christ' and 'with Christ.' All that seemed to matter to her, as she looked back over her life and gave us glimpses into her memory, was that Christ had redeemed her and marked her as His own. This was demonstrated in how she lived, right up until her final illness ... What mattered was the reality of her relationship with Christ and its eternal significance." What do the people who know you see you caring the most about?

Jack Turner
Truth in the Arctic
David Luckman

Jack Turner was trained pharmacist and pastor who went to the arctic to translate God's Word into the native language. It was a world of snow and hunting and anyone who lived there had to become familiar with the ways of living in the arctic. Ten weeks out of every year the sun never set and for three months the world was in complete darkness.

The spiritual darkness of the North was being pushed back by the power of the Gospel and the Lord Jesus Christ that Jack Turner followed. But danger is around every corner in the wild North – and Jack runs into trouble.

ISBN: 978-1-5271-0792-2

OTHER BOOKS IN THE TRAIL BLAZERS SERIES

Augustine, The Truth Seeker
ISBN 978-1-78191-296-6
John Calvin, After Darkness Light
ISBN 978-1-78191-550-9
Fanny Crosby, The Blind Girl's Song
ISBN 978-1-78191-163-1
John Knox, The Sharpened Sword
ISBN 978-1-78191-057-3
Eric Liddell, Finish the Race
ISBN 978-1-84550-590-5
Martin Luther, Reformation Fire
ISBN 978-1-78191-521-9
Robert Moffat, Africa's Brave Heart
ISBN 978-1-84550-715-2
D.L. Moody, One Devoted Man
ISBN 978-1-78191-676-6
Mary of Orange, At the Mercy of Kings
ISBN 978-1-84550-818-0
Patrick of Ireland: The Boy who Forgave
ISBN: 978-1-78191-677-3
John Stott, The Humble Leader
ISBN 978-1-84550-787-9
Ulrich Zwingli, Shepherd Warrior
ISBN 978-1-78191-803-6

For a full list of Trail Blazers, please see our website: www.christianfocus.com
All Trail Blazers are available as e-books

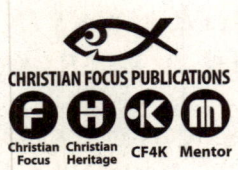

Christian Focus Publications publishes books for adults and children under its four main imprints: Christian Focus, CF4K, Mentor and Christian Heritage. Our books reflect our conviction that God's Word is reliable and Jesus is the way to know him, and live for ever with him.

Our children's publication list covers pre-school to early teens. We also publish personal and family devotional titles, biographies and inspirational stories that children will love.

From pre-school board books to teenage apologetics, we have it covered!

**Find us at our web page:
www.christianfocus.com**